Sisters Around the World

The Global Struggle for Female Equality

Trudie M. Eklund

Hamilton Books
an imprint of
UNIVERSITY PRESS OF AMERICA,® INC.
Dallas • Lanham • Boulder • New York • Oxford

Hamilton Books
4501 Forbes Boulevard
Suite 200
Lanham, Maryland 20706
UPA Acquisitions Department (301) 459-3366

PO Box 317
Oxford
OX2 9RU, UK

Library of Congress Control Number: 2004100645
ISBN 0-7618-2819-2 (paperback : alk. ppr.)

Contents

Introduction

The study of cultures has always fascinated me and for many years my husband and I have enjoyed the opportunity to travel extensively. While playing the tourist and enjoying the sights and sounds of numerous countries I, not unlike many travelers, initially made mental notes on the cultural characteristics that divide us. But there is more to travel than that. The more I researched the cultures I became aware of the fact that women's lives across the world are in many ways very similar.

Thus this book came into being and enabled me to relive many of our travels while doing research. My thanks goes to my husband, Eric for his research, suggestions, patience and encouragement as each chapter came together.

I also received a wealth of information from The United States Committee for the United Nations Development Fund for Women (UNIFEM). Unfortunately women and children make up 70 percent of the world's poor, yet women perform ⅔ of the world's work. Women produce, process and market ⅗ of all the world's food and yet still comprise over ⅔ of the world's illiterate population. While we are now well into the new millennium, women in developing countries remain victims of violence in ⅓ of all families.

It is estimated that when UNIFEM helps 250,000 women, 1,000,000 children benefit, thus a family is changed. It is my hope that the accounts in this book will help to bring a new awareness to the gender inequality that stretches across the globe.

Prologue

This book speaks to all women around the world. To the urban woman in a highly industrialized society engaged in the high-tech world of computers, fax machines and cell phones facing down gender discrimination and dedicated to shattering the glass ceiling while busily engaged in raising a family and keeping her marriage on track (unsuccessfully at times). To the rural woman in a third world country whose first need is basic survival all the while coping with ancient customs rooted in her culture that considers women chattel and inferior beings who at best are tolerated, controlled, and beaten (if necessary) while birthing and raising children.

What unites us, females of the species who practice a vast array of spiritual beliefs and rituals and who have different political persuasions? What many-layered thread binds us all with varying skin colors from white to brown to black, who speak different languages, with an assortment of educational backgrounds and whose economic levels range from a culture of plenty to a culture of scarcity? What dynamics obliterate our cultural differences and instead fuses us together as we make our way along life's path from birth to puberty to motherhood to old age and death without ever having met, talked and comforted each other?

It is male domination and misogyny and the plethora of problems that it creates across the globe. Gender stereotypes have remained pervasive through the centuries and are still present in our "modern world" as females lives' continue to be hemmed in by kitchens and office walls but most of all by narrow debilitating, destructive and demeaning prejudices against the "weaker sex." Today, perhaps more than ever women's indomitable spirit hungers for a more complete menu of options for their lives and the accounts that are contained in this book give evidence that there are no boundaries to what women can dream and what they can achieve. They are not just mere survivors but successful survivors as they overcome hurdles that would have destroyed a weaker sex.

The trauma of desertion and resulting homelessness for Margie in the United States is analogous to the pain and rejection the Malawian woman Chantal feels as she attempts to work her way through widowhood and family abandonment. Tawanna struggles to overcome a bloody assault and rape not far from her home in Abuja, Nigeria. Her condition runs parallel to the heartbreaking situation a young Greek woman, Melina finds herself in after being tossed aside by a member of the clergy and who must raise their child, a product of their affair, by herself. The pain of domestic violence a Guatemalan man inflicts on his wife, Elga is similar to the deep physical and emotional abuse an Irish husband thousands of miles away imposes on his mate, Nona. In Sicily Teresa's situation after enduring years of overbearing commands and discouragement from her husband is not unlike the obstacles Larisa from Russia must work through as she strains to seize an opportunity to further her dancing career contrary to the wishes and demands of her husband. A young Spanish woman, Olivia, dreams of higher education in spite of her father's dictates that higher education is only for the family's male members. Her dreams are akin to the aspirations of a young woman, Celia from Peru who longs to do the unthinkable for her economic and gender class and learn to read. The heartbroken mother in Romania, Ana, grieves the loss of a daughter to complications arising from AIDS. Her agony is matched by Maya, the family's only breadwinner, who returns to her Chinese village and is overcome with guilt and sorrow at her father's death from Hepatitis and her mother's fatal illness caused by Tuberculosis, both the result of weakened immune systems due to AIDS. The pain of her husband's failing health and her impending widowhood is compounded for Margie in the United States who must face chauvinism in the work place that is so insidious that as a last resort she prepares to file a law suit to obtain her promotion, an upgrade she has waited eighteen long years for. And lastly, perhaps we can recognize a little of ourselves in Gena when she becomes conscious of the strengths deep inside her.

For many of these women it is the initial connection with others of their gender, some in comparable situations, that provides them with place to talk, listen and shed a tear or two if need be. The resulting camaraderie affords them the support and nurturing they need to face their day-to-day struggles with relationships laden with hostility and control. The nurturing given so freely furthers the process and uncovers the strengths (that some may never have thought they possessed) to cast off their subordinate and denigrated role and reinvent themselves. These women have learned not to make peace with male dominance but rather to be satisfied with no less than equal and valued status. They take pride and celebrate resplendently not only their own accomplishments but the successes of their sisters as they reach a new level of thinking and economic independence.

Feminism means looking at the world with an altered perspective to observe and analyze the critical issues facing all women everywhere. *Sisters Around The World* is a series of divergent portraits that brings us into the subtle and not so subtle transformations that are occurring on our planet as women overcome their insecurities and declare that we will not walk behind men, instead we will walk beside them and all of humankind will be the better for it.

Chapter One

"There is in every true woman's heart a spark of heavenly fire, which lies dormant in the broad daylight of prosperity, but which kindles up and beams and blazes in the dark hour of adversity."

—Washington Irving

The first rays of sunlight had barely appeared on the horizon when the thud of boxes plummeting to the floor awoke Stacy with a start. Jim, her husband of eight years was hurrying though the room grabbing his things for a trip to California. The temperature had dropped well below freezing during the night and the radio warned of an early winter storm heading east from the mountains. Denver would get doused with at least "seven to ten inches of snow before nightfall." Stacy would have loved to linger under the soft down comfort but too much had to be done today.

As she made her way to the kitchen she murmured a silent prayer that the previous evening wouldn't be repeated. But she knew differently. It had been the same day after day, the arguments, the name-calling and the tears. Nothing seemed to be going right for them since they had been laid off from their well-paying jobs. Denver was not unlike other American cities that were facing an economic slowdown. First Jim had arrived home disheartened and woozy from a stop off at the country club's bar and waving his pink slip. When a well-known brokerage house announced it was downsizing due to the nation's lackluster economy Jim became one of twenty-seven employees leaving their desks for the last time. Within a few weeks Stacy's job was in jeopardy also. Rumor had it that the advertising company where she was employed was in deep financial trouble and to cut costs and save the agency several employees were laid off. Within days Stacy was presented with her dreaded pink dismissal form.

At first they appeared not to be unduly concerned and continued their somewhat lavish lifestyle as before. True, fate had thrown them a curve but before long their lives would be back to normal—they were sure of it. They'd never lacked for money. Shortly after Jim graduated from California's prestigious Pepperdine University with a master's degree in business and finance he moved to Denver and settled into a position at a highly successful brokerage house. During the bull market of the 1980's he learned to live the good life especially after he was elevated to vice-president. On the first day of a company outing to the Vail ski slopes a tall attractive young woman with thick black hair and striking green eyes caught Jim's attention. They rode to the top of Vail Mountain on the tram together and enjoyed racing down the slopes in sight of each other. For the remainder of the weekend they were inseparable and through the rest of the winter and spring their long distance romance blossomed. Some weekends Jim would fly to Manhattan and other weekends Stacy would arrive in Denver to catch the last snows of the season. By early summer they were engaged and involved in planning their wedding.

Stacy had graduated from the City College of New York and loved the sights, the sounds and the smells of Manhattan. Before she'd met Jim she had no intention of ever leaving the city. She had plenty of friends, was involved in a mentoring program at City College and enjoyed a good salary from her satisfying position at a top-notch Madison Avenue advertising firm. When Jim asked her to move to Denver and be his wife, she gave the decision a lot of thought before agreeing to uproot herself. It would be a decision that would haunt her during the troublesome years ahead.

Soon after their wedding Jim and Stacy moved into a comfortable and elegant Denver townhouse and purchased a condo in Vail. Their ample salaries provided them membership in an upscale country club, two new cars and a recently purchased SUV for mountain driving. They enjoyed expensive clothes and even on 'dress-down' Fridays they both left the house impeccably dressed. Credit card bills weren't a problem they attempted to keep the balances "within a safe limit." The mortgage payment on the condo in Vail was never in arrears nor was the payment on their city dwelling. But severance pay goes only so far and as the weeks and months dragged on more and more bills were left unpaid. It was when the bill collectors began hounding them on a daily basis that Jim decided to leave for California. He had always loved the high Sierras and anyway he told Stacy "I'll find a job out there. You sell everything here and we'll start over. Don't worry. I'll call you."

It bothered Stacy, actually it bothered her a great deal that she would be left alone to answer all the bill collectors and some nights they argued over Jim's plan well into the early morning hours but her husband wouldn't be dissuaded. After a quick cup of coffee he packed his things into the SUV and ignored her last plea to allow her to accompany him to California. After a hurried good-by the door slammed behind him and silence filled the house.

Sleet began to dance across the windows and the rooms seemed to be getting colder as Stacy headed for the wall safe in the bedroom closet. When she counted the money her heart fell. Jim had filled his pockets and left little for her. She remembered that she had planned to bring many of her designer clothes to a resale shop in the afternoon but instead she crawled between the sheets and fell into a fitful sleep. It would be one of the many nights and days she'd spend trying to escape into the darkness of sleep after drowning her worries in a bottle of wine.

Before the house phone and cell phones were canceled Stacy occasionally heard from her husband but when she did their curt conversations did little to lift her spirits. The crisis that could have brought them even closer had divided them and the void between them was deepening rapidly. Jim seemed to be another person, so distant and so aloof. He no longer inquired about the bill collectors and appeared to care little that most of their furniture was gone and on consignment at an up-scale furniture company. Stacy felt as if they were in separate rowboats on a dark and mysterious sea drifting father and farther apart. Jim was vague about looking for a job, vague about where he was living and vague about their future. They argued and finally he reluctantly gave her a phone number where he could be reached. After their conversations Stacy usually folded into a bottle of wine. More and more her days and nights were filled with alcohol.

One snowy morning Stacy peered from the window and stared at the car tracks in the fresh snow, the last vestige of their automobiles that had just been repossessed. With their possessions vanishing and the wall safe lying open and empty Stacy was slowly sinking into a pit of depression a malady that had followed her through life whether she had a reason to be despondent or not. She remembered her mother, at times cheerful and busy, her eyes sparkling as she spoke and laughed noisily after emerging from a bout of depression when she had drawn the draperies and existed in an empty world of darkness for days or weeks. Stacy hated to come home from school during those times. When she peeked into her mother's silent dark bedroom she vowed she'd never live like that. And for the most part she didn't live like her mother had. Whenever she felt the melancholy taking over she'd make a special effort to overcome it and usually within a short time she was back to her usual self. But now she lacked the ability to escape the hand of despair clutching her tightly in its grasp.

The weeks dragged by with no word from Jim. Still the hope flickered deep inside her that he'd write soon with glowing details of his new job and before long she'd be heading westward. As the city glistened under the holiday lights made more dramatic by the gently falling snow Stacy became more and more disheartened. Her eyes scanned the empty rooms and the nearly empty closets and her tears fell. She remembered the impressive paintings they had hung, the fine mahogany furniture that had given the house an elegant and comfortable look and the colorful oriental rugs that topped the parquet floors. All of it was gone, most of it to make a partial payment on the townhouse's mortgage. The condo in Vail sold fairly quickly but all Stacy was left with was a few hundred dollars. Probably what she missed most however was the luxurious king size comfortable bed. Now she slept every night on the cold bare floor in a sleeping bag topped with her down comfort.

As Thanksgiving neared Stacy collected her coins and headed for a pay phone in an attempt to contact Jim. What she heard caused her to almost stop breathing. A man's voice on the other end had dropped a bomb.

"Yeah, Jim lived there. He worked a few weeks and then all of a sudden he up an' announced he was leaving. Something about breaking the bank in Vegas." He gave a chuckle and added, "Ah, he was just a crazy happy–go-lucky guy he probably didn't mean it."

At that moment it hit Stacy that she was totally and helplessly alone. During their years together she'd learned that more than once in his life Jim had fallen victim to compulsive gambling. Her heart would skip a beat when they were with friends and Jim would make his usual suggestion.

"Let's have a good old-fashioned card game, the higher the stakes the better."

Later on he'd refuse to admit how much money he'd lost and the ride home was made in stony silence.

A few days after the Thanksgiving holiday, Stacy wearing an extra layer of clothing (she had sold her coats) and with what pride she had left carried several more clothes and jewelry to the resale shop. Before entering she lingered outside, her face pressing into the window. Customers lighthearted and chattering were busily combing through the racks searching for that special dress or suit for a Christmas gathering or a posh New Year's Eve party. Stacy turned to leave—she couldn't jostle around in the shop when it was jammed with all those happy customers but the hunger pains and the thought of another bottle of wine forced her to reconsider. A half-hour later she left the shop with a fistful of money and felt she could survive for a little while longer.

She made a quick stop at a corner liquor store before heading for her bus stop. While she waited her eye caught sight of a pitiful old woman picking through the trash cans in an alley behind the shops and restaurants. The old woman trudged along pushing a dented and lopsided shopping cart no doubt filled with her meager possessions. Stacy watched her until she was out of sight. The image of that woman would haunt her. It was as if it had been burned into her brain. The old woman was everywhere. When Stacy lay starring at the blank walls her head fuzzy from the wine the image was there. When Stacy folded into her sleeping bag she felt as if the woman was beside her. The old woman was the first image to greet her in the morning when she awoke. Stacy wouldn't or perhaps couldn't have admitted it to herself then but she was heading down the same path.

With the holidays fast approaching Stacy was sinking more and more into fear and despair and she hated how it felt. She remembered her mother's behavior when she couldn't face life and following in her footsteps Stacy closed the draperies, barricaded the door with a leftover chest and told herself that she was safe from the outside world and all its problems but none of it worked. Some days she was too despondent to crawl out of her sleeping bag and stumble to the kitchen for a cup of coffee. Many evenings starring at the cold black sky she thought of suicide and wondered if it was the answer. Was this how her mother had felt years earlier when she had died by her own hand? When Stacy caught a glimpse of herself in the bathroom mirror she was sure the image facing her was a mad woman. Her hair was matted and dirty, her eyes appeared sunken and her skin was an ashy gray.

The week after New Year's Stacy clicked open the wall safe, counted all her money and mustered enough courage and strength to leave the house. Stopping at the mailbox she thumbed through the bills and junk mail hoping against hope that there would be a letter, a card, something, anything from Jim. When there wasn't, in a rage she flung the envelopes and circulars into the trash without noticing that there was a long brown envelope with a copy of a legal document announcing the mortgage company's deadline to foreclose on the townhouse. The sheriff would be serving papers and the house was to be boarded up. For the young woman things were beginning to unravel in a hurry.

Stacy had been in the small market hundreds of times but now the aisles blurred together in a haze. Prices were hop-scotching through her mind and she found she couldn't even add up the cost of her few groceries. She wasn't alone. Someone was watching her with piercing brown eyes that flashed when he noticed the small wad of bills in Stacy's hand. He was another one of those living on the margins of society and for him it was plain and simple. She had money and he was going to take it.

Lingering by the store's large window his eyes remained glued on Stacy while she made her way to the cashier and out the door. She was too busy stuffing the change carefully into her pockets to notice the dark foreboding figure closing in behind her. In a flash she was shoved into an alley, thrown to the ground, beaten and robbed of her money and all her groceries. The figure gave her one last kick and disappeared down the alley. A police unit answering a security call a few yards away found her sitting dazed at the same spot she had fallen. They lifted her to her feet and attempted to take her to a hospital emergency room but she stubbornly refused. She cringed when she heard their radio report to the police station.

"Not much going on this end—just another bag lady robbed."

Then they left the scene without even a backward glance. Every last trickle of energy had left her and she was physically and emotionally drained. She had no groceries and no bus fare to get home, which in retrospect was probably best. If she had gone to her house she would have seen the sheriff nailing a paper to the door and a locksmith changing the locks. She'd often wondered as a child if there was such a place as heaven or such a place as hell and what it would be like. Now she felt as if she was already in hell. She felt totally powerless. The path was clear, she was either going to end up spending the frigid nights on the streets or go to a shelter as the police had suggested.

On a quiet tree lined street within a short walking distance from the downtown's tall office buildings Stacy stood outside one of the city's homeless shelters and hesitated before pushing the door opened. Was this reality or was the life she had lived several months ago reality? She wasn't sure. Inside she entered a long dingy hallway with a discolored light bulb and bent socket dangling from a frayed electrical cord. The place had a strong unpleasant odor of disinfectant. An open door led her to an office where an older man with shiny white hair and a pleasant smile sat behind a desk. He must have heard the story a hundred times. Stacy with no place to go was still in denial.

"I only need a room for tonight."

He listened patiently and nodded in agreement as the young woman continued.

"I'll be hearing from my husband soon."

Attempting to appear nonchalant she added, "if I don't I'll just go to Vegas and find him."

She couldn't admit to herself that she didn't have the money to go anywhere. She soon learned the shelter's routine. Most of the first and second floors were sleeping quarters for those unfortunates who roamed the streets during the day while wondering where they'd spend the night. No one could stake out a cot before 7 P.M. On those nights when the shelter filled rapidly many transients were carted to another site by city buses. The sleeping quarters were full of men and women some chronically homeless while others were the working poor gainfully employed but without adequate funds to make it on their own. Disputes and clashes occurred with little provocation and the stress level seemed to be highest just before lights out at 10 P.M. All of them appeared to sleep with one eye opened as they guarded their few tattered possessions.

The third and fourth floors housed families with children who were bused to and from school. They were a ragtag lot with worry and hunger written all over their faces. They ate breakfast and lunch at school and it wasn't unusual to hear them tell their mother, "I'm so hungry." Often Stacy, not meaning to eavesdrop, still overheard their pitiful question.

"Moma, do we have to live here forever and ever?"

A play yard situated in the back of the building where any sense of peace was just an illusion was the scene of many scuffles over a toy. Some children took their frustration out on basketballs that never seemed to be properly inflated. Others just stood and starred at the ground their thoughts perhaps drifting back to better times. The 'lights out' bell rang exactly at 10 P.M. and the shelter emptied at 7 A.M. when a cleaning crew descended to mop, scrub and prepare the building for another night.

Stacy became part of the little army standing in line for meal tickets that could be redeemed at any of three fast food restaurants lining the downtown streets. But eating there was another challenge to one's self-esteem. The down-and-outers had to enter the restaurant through a side door and remain isolated from the general public in a crowded, less than clean stuffy side room. After breakfast the homeless fanned out through the streets searching trash cans for anything they could eat or use. With little possessions to call their own, it was pathetic what they picked up and fought over and with anger in their eyes could be heard screaming, "don't touch that, that's mine." As the morning wore on they usually ended up in a city park wrapped in tattered clothing, sleeping on benches or eyeing the office workers scurrying to the warmth of their buildings.

Stacy remembered when she'd been one of them, enjoying her days working on advertising projects and nights with Jim building dreams about their future over a bottle of expensive wine at one of the upscale restaurants a short drive from their house. Every time she glanced westward to the beautiful snowcapped mountains her thoughts returned to the pleasant ski trips they'd had the previous winter. Life was fun then, now each day was a challenge just to survive. She ate, walked and talked as if in a trance and spent most of her days wandering the downtown streets. At night she'd return to the shelter exhausted and slumped over with fatigue. One evening she was especially despondent as she reached the shelter. Minutes before as the late afternoon sun was beginning to sink behind the mountains an especially well-dressed woman threw Stacy a $1.00 and sneered.

"You're a disgrace. Get off the streets and get yourself a job."

She hated the woman for saying that and when she looked in a store window she hated herself. Her clothes were rumpled and dirty, her hair hadn't been combed in days and she couldn't remember when she had washed. The showers at the shelter had no curtains and Stacey bristled at the lack of privacy.

Now she realized that she just plain smelled bad and for the rest of the week Stacy couldn't shake the feeling of being totally worthless.

The days were becoming somewhat warmer which allowed the snow mounds to melt during the sunny afternoons only to refreeze during the night as the temperatures fell. It was on one such morning that Stacy on her way to breakfast slipped on the hard ice and fell back into the street before oncoming traffic. Had it not been for two quick thinking bystanders who yanked her up Stacy would have been seriously injured or worse. A policeman joined the crowd that had gathered and called for an ambulance. She'd refused a hospital visit before but now thinking she had no control over her life anyway she closed her eyes and slipped into a dark place.

At the emergency room nurses and doctors fussed over her and attempted to get her to speak. Where did she hurt—her legs—her back—her head? Where did she live? On and on they questioned but she would have none of it and remained silent which prompted a call to the hospital's Mental Health Unit. Following her evaluation she was deposited on the psychiatric floor and for the first time in weeks she was warm and she was comfortable. The sheets and blankets were fresh and soft against her body, the pillowcase smelled of mountain air and she slowly drifted into a restful sleep. When she awoke the next morning a nurse with a kind face and gentle hands was urging her to eat.

By the end of the week Stacy was slowly inching out of her shell and began to feel connected. She and the day nurse Jodi had become friends and even shared a few laughs, which made Stacy realize how much she had missed at the shelter. Even though some of the same people spent their nights together week after week, few people spoke or even acknowledged each other. They were living in their own little cocoon of illusion and despair. On the streets or in the park people passed by and not only did they not speak, they avoided all eye contact and at times Stacy felt she had to be invisible.

Nurses, doctors and mental health workers came and went and Stacy couldn't avoid the inevitable much longer, she had to open her life to them. When she began the words came in torrents. She recounted her mother's frequent bouts of depression and changeable behavior. She revisited her mother's suicide and admitted that she too had been suicidal. She relived her life as a promising advertising agent, as a bubbly and happy and then deserted wife, and as a pitiful bag lady. Slowly and painfully she began to shed the cloak of embarrassment and guilt for living on the streets that had been smothering her. And slowly and painfully she began to question her judgment of Jim and admitted to herself that he hadn't been all the things she'd thought he was. Slowly and painfully her thoughts darted back to her satisfying life in Manhattan and she wondered if she'd ever be able to pick up the shards of her shattered life and be content again.

She was making progress however. One afternoon was especially insightful when one of her doctors called her a survivor and wondered aloud how many others would have done any differently given the set of circumstances she had lived through. She felt as if she could laugh and talk all night after hearing that. Actually many days she felt unusually lighthearted and wanted to laugh and giggle without any provocation. As the days went on she found that she enjoyed the hospital routine. Every morning accompanied by Jodi she'd make her way to the psychiatrist's office. After several sessions she became familiar with the term "Bipolar Affective Disorder" and was put on a regimen of medicine to keep her emotions on an even keel. It was a routine that she adhered to faithfully.

After an unusually lengthy session with the hospital's chief psychiatrist Stacy learned that she would soon be discharged and moved to a group home. In a carefully tailored message he held her hand before he spoke.

"It's time for you to move on, Stacy."

A sense of panic gripped her. The hospital had been her safe haven, how could she live without the security she'd felt there? Back in her room Jodi tried to assure her.

"We'll still be friends. You'll have more freedom there and we'll meet for lunch on my days off and maybe take in a movie."

The morning of her departure from the hospital would live in her mind forever. From early morning the small sunny room was crammed with nurses and other staff who trickled in to say good-by. There was much hugging and smiles and well wishes through the tears but the thing that struck Stacy the most was the new dark blue and red fleece pantsuit, shoes, coat and sweater that the nurses had chipped-to buy for her and she wondered how she could ever repay them. She couldn't have know it then but fate had a few more surprises in store for her.

It began slowly of course, Stacy settling into the grand old red brick building set back from the street. The three-story architecture spoke of a grander time when visitors no doubt arrived by horse and carriage. The huge gently swaying willow trees already beginning to bud in the warm springtime weather gave the grounds a certain stately look. The ample patio and gardens to the back divided the main building that housed the females from another larger building reserved for the men. A list of chores and events was posted in the well-used stainless steel over-sized kitchen and word had it that attendance was required at all group therapy meetings. The twice a week sessions were never run-of-the-mill gatherings and although each member was encouraged to speak it wasn't mandatory. Some attendees were wrestling with alcohol and/or drug addiction while others were attempting to cope with other deep psychological problems. At times they attended in a state of euphoria and other days they were mired in deep depression and sat stiffly while staring at the floor unflinchingly. While the group therapy lessons were a chance to mingle Stacy usually kept to herself. Most of her free time was spent in the computer room working on developing new graphics and advertising logos. She was beginning to think of her future, living on her own and rebuilding her career. The computer room was where she was one heavily overcast afternoon when the manager announced that she had a caller.

Lisa Kempt with long beige hair and ocean-blue eyes was Jodi's friend. The two young women lived in the same apartment building and built a friendship through the years. Jodi had spoken to Lisa about Stacy's experiences and Lisa, a journalist for a local newspaper, began to envision the possibilities of exposing the underside of homelessness from an articulate woman who had nowhere else to turn but the streets. They spent many hours talking and a few weeks later the newspaper was on the newsstands or being delivered to thousands of homes and businesses in the area. No one was prepared for what was to come.

It would be difficult to recount the exact time each event occurred, they all seemed to blend together. A businesswomen's club at their next luncheon voted to create a fund for Stacy and the area's other homeless women. Not too many weeks later several citizens' groups whose mission was social action organized new groups to lobby the state legislature to set aside funds for affordable housing for the working poor and there was some hope that some legislation would eventually make its way successfully through the system. The call went out to those church groups already caring for the street dwellers to increase their numbers; some did and eventually even redoubled their efforts. As time went on new kitchens were opened and additional feeding vans canvassed the streets and the fears that the interest in the homeless would peak and then dissipate appeared groundless. Stacy conquered her nervousness and appeared on TV. She never tired of speaking of the children, those one in four youngsters in the nation whose bleak childhood means standing in line in a soup kitchen all the while wondering if they will get enough to eat each day. To emphasize the plight of the poverty-stricken she'd look straight into the TV camera.

"People think they can image what living on the street really is—they don't know, they can't begin to know unless they live through it themselves. Whatever pride one has is slowly eroded. Some days I didn't even care if I lived or died. I had nothing."

While most of the city residents had been aware of the street people it was Stacy who had given a name and face to the problem and for that she was feted at luncheons and other civic gatherings. As the community pulled together Stacy received other offers of assistance. She received legal advice from a large law firm who paid for an investigator to find Jim. A month later Stacy received a report with the bare facts, "said subject is living with a cocktail waitress in a posh apartment near the outskirts of Las Vegas." She read the report a few times and hardly shed a tear before folding it carefully and tucking it in a drawer. Stacy now felt it was time to move on.

A well-placed call to her old boss at the Manhattan advertising agency brought a song to her heart. Her old job was waiting for her. With a loan from a women's group she purchased a plane ticket. As she leaned back in her seat and watched the clouds floating lazily by so many memories churned through her head. She'd never forget the women who had been her benefactors; it wasn't just empathy at a distance, they had stepped in and taken her into their hearts and while championing her cause they were also championing the cause of other women caught in the same predicament.

These women and others like them are part of all the world's sisters marching together devoting their time and efforts to give comfort, strength and encouragement to those of their gender who at least one time in their lives feel that they have reached the end of their rope.

Chapter Two

"Sometime in your life you will go on a journey. It will be the longest journey you have ever taken. It is the journey to find yourself."

— Katherine Sharp

Chantal was awake before the golden light of the sun signaled a new day. She was full of excitement, today was going to be so very special. Albion her husband was returning from the bush and she had wonderful news for him. She had suspected she was pregnant soon after he left with several government and business officials to travel the countryside to inspect and report on the nation's staple crop, maize. It was no secret throughout this southeast African country that famine was threatening the population's very existence. Daily reports told of mounting deaths in the villages due to starvation and the hunger crisis, deemed to be the worst ever, was now creeping towards Malawi's largest city, Blantyre where Chantal and Albion lived.

Compared to the rest of the population their life was tipped with gold. Albion's job afforded them a mid-size, well kept house on a clean tree lined street with an indoor bathroom and an adequate garden. Their neighbors were government officials and top and middle management officers of the few foreign companies with investments in Malawi. Albion and Chantal had taken pride in their home which was neat and well furnished. They ate well, what they couldn't find in the city's main markets was provided by their well-kept garden or bartered with their little tight-knit community of friends. But as with all seemingly perfect lives, their life together had a flaw.

In their three years of marriage, much to her chagrin Chantal had suffered two miscarriages and had failed to produce the child that both of them longed for. But this time it would be different. She had gone to a doctor the day before and while the city's medical facilities were barely basic, in the rural areas they were more often than not, completely non-existent. She felt better than she had in her earlier pregnancies and she was free of the cramps that had plagued her before.

The sun was already hot in the blue sky when Chantal rose to meet the day. The neighborhood was coming alive, people waving good-by and heading for work and children walking to school laughing and joking with their friends. In this seemingly normal setting one would never know that these children were the lucky ones — over half of Malawian children aged five and above are not receiving any kind of schooling. And in this seemingly normal setting one would never know that just a few short kilometers away, people were rising from the places they had slept, on pallets or on the bare ground, wondering if they'd have any food at all for the day. Sadly one would never known that over the next hill, what little water was available for cooking and drinking was parasite ridden and unsafe. In this seemingly normal setting one could not have known that less than a half-days walk, an eerie silence had fallen over several settlements due to a cholera outbreak that had snuffed out the lives of hundreds. According to health officials the disease was spreading rapidly especially to those whose resistance to the waterborne disease was lessened by malnutrition and HIV/AIDS.

Chantal searched her closet for her most colorful finery. Albion had always liked the vivid red one, dappled with shades of yellow and marked with intricate circles and geometric lines. She'd spend hours on her hair, weaving it under her turban. Her make-up would indicate to a passerby that today was a happy day. Before the heat of the day set in she went to the garden to gather a few sweet potatoes to boil and mix with peanuts to make Albion's favorite dish.

More than once she glanced at the clock. She must have gone to the door a hundred times, her eyes scanning the landscape for any sign of Albion or the men he'd traveled with. And always she'd turn and slump into a chair disappointed. The afternoon dragged on and with the temperature rising, the house was becoming uncomfortably hot. She'd never liked the hot season and always looked forward to November when the rains came and cooled the air. She let her mind wander; her baby would be born before the rainy season ended in April. She ran her hand across her stomach and wondered if it was a boy or a girl. In the sublime happiness of the moment she imagined a happy little face with plump cheeks and smiling eyes. She knew that Albion had often spoke of wanting many children and many sons. She chuckled to herself when she thought of the wonderful time that they'd have deciding on a name for their firstborn. Yes, life was good. In this seemingly perfect setting she could not have known that disaster was fast approaching.

The hands of the clock barely seemed to budge as Chantal vacillated between impatience "he should be home by now" to worry "hope everything's all right" to joy at the news Albion would hear. An ominous silence seemed to drift through the house until suddenly without warning Chantal was startled by a sharp knock on the door and a policeman with a stern cold look walked inside. The next few moments would be burned in her memory forever. The policeman sat down—she sat down. The policeman tried to speak—she tried to make small talk. Finally he hushed her and in a terse voice began.

"You know that our country has the highest rate of road accidents in southeastern Africa . . . three people were killed just this morning . . . in fact a couple hours ago . . . their bus overturned on one of those rutted and jagged roads outside the city." He drew in a deep breath and continued. "Your husband was one of the three."

Chantel screamed, she cried, she beat her chest but nothing stopped the pain. The policeman stayed all the while his eyes fixed on the floor, then departed to summon Albion's parents. Thus Chantal was totally alone to deal with her sorrow, her despair, her anger and her helplessness. At times she sobbed; at times she felt numb and was unable to cry. Disjointed thoughts flashed through her mind. Perhaps it hadn't happened. Perhaps the afternoon had just been a bad dream, Albion would be home any minute and she'd hear the sound of him calling her name. Then harsh reality would set in and she'd repeat the same range of emotions, sorrow, despair, anger and helplessness.

Friends, hearing the news, drifted in and out the remainder of the afternoon and most of the evening endeavoring to comfort her but she could not be comforted. Her world had collapsed and she was sinking into a dark hole of hopelessness. Before the sun set for the day Albion's parents, Davon and Iyabode arrived and soon Chantal's now ex-mother-in-law was taking charge of the situation. First she concocted a powerful potion for her grieving ex-daughter-in-law. Before the brew took effect Chantal remembered her ex-in-laws roaming through the house, methodically opening closets and searching bureau drawers. The potion caused her to float in and out of consciousness before she had time to question them and that was where she remained for the rest of the week. She couldn't have known that Iyabode and Davon had seized upon an opportunity that would make their lives better but would devastate hers.

With their ex-daughter-in-law oblivious to what was happening, Albion's parents took charge of his funeral according to their own tribal customs. Chantal couldn't have known that they were more concerned about keeping her in a stupor than having her awake and interfering with their plans. She'd remember later Iyabode bending over her at regular intervals with her curt order, "drink more of this." But the day would finally arrive when her ex-in-laws were ready for Chantal to be wide-awake to hear what they had determined.

As with many poor cultures that find themselves drowning in extreme poverty with no immediate hope of bettering their lot in life, the huge gap between those with a reasonably comfortable life and those with nothing gave rise to the ancient custom of Dispossession. Kinship in Malawi as in many other cultures is defined paterlineally as it has been for centuries and while property grabbing is accepted, the practice always escalates during particularly hard times. Thus if a son dies, his family no longer feels any responsibility to his widow and children, if any. Further, any assets that the son and his wife accumulated during his lifetime become the assets of his family. The hard fact was that Chantal had become a trespasser, an interloper in her own home.

Iyabode and Davon were well aware of the custom and they viewed the death of their son as an opportunity to better their lives. Fearing the publicity that the practice had received in the past few months with Malawians speaking out on the hardships Dispossession caused widows and children, they felt an urgency to act immediately. Chantal tried to reason with them but her ex-in-laws would have none of it. Instead of talking Iyabode and Davon, unusually grim-faced shoved her towards the door with only a basket holding a few of her clothes. The remainder of her wardrobe and all the household items that Chantel and Albion had so lovingly accumulated would be sold to bring the ex-in-laws much needed money.

With few options for her in the city, Chantal decided to return to her village. She thought of her mother, always loving, always giving warmth and comfort to the family and her father stubbornly working the parched land even in times of acute drought. It wouldn't be easy adjusting to life in the remote settlement of her birth, she had enjoyed life in the city, but she decided she'd stay with her parents until her baby was born. Whenever she thought of her baby the heartbreak of all that had happened seemed to lesson somewhat. With her few possessions tucked into the basket on top of her head she turned her back on Blantyre and never looked back. She could never have imagined that her journey would take her to a most unlikely destination.

As Chantal headed west towards her parent's village, she faced numbers of people heading east, toward the city buoyed with the belief that life would be better there than in the bush. Nowhere was the line between urban and rural more evident than beyond the outskirts of the city. The deeper she got into the bush the worse the conditions were. Open trenches were full of thick sewerage drawing drones of flies, the scent of decaying refuse filled the air and the fields that had been planted by subsistence farmers year in and year out lay idle. The soil had suffered through cycles of intense drought and flooding rains and most tragic of all, many of the most productive members of the communities were unable to plant or harvest due to the diseases making swift inroads into the population.

She realized now why Albion had been so concerned with the meager harvest. Many nights after she'd gone to bed he'd work well into the early morning hours pouring over mounds of paper work spread across the kitchen table. The agriculture reports were unnerving to say the least. Small farms that once had been productive providing potatoes and root vegetables enough for several families were deserted. Not far from starvation many villagers were resorting to eating unripened maize or grass further compounding their health problems.

Fearful of criminals who roamed the countryside at night, Chantel discovered a field a safe distance from the road to sleep and the first light of dawn found her eager to continue her trek. Each new day was similar to the day before. She continued to trudge along in the thick heat, past large cracks in the ground where streams had once flowed, past burly tobacco fields, tea plantations and rows of cotton fields operated by a few lucky families who had owned the land for generations. She skirted settlements with teetering shacks that once had been full of laughing and joyous children, now almost empty of people.

The trip seemed endless and the day came when Chantal could no longer continue her walking. She had always been the picture of dignity and strength walking erect, now her shoulders sagged. At first she tried to ignore it rationalizing that the cramping was just a result of everything that had happened and her pains would disappear as soon as she reached the village. Several miles from the settlement she dropped by the side of the road, sick and feverish. By now her cramps had become short grabbing pains and she couldn't stop retching. She watched the sun drop behind blue gray clouds and suddenly there was an unfamiliar coolness to the air. At first she thought her clothes were wet because of an all-to-short burst of rain but the flood of wetness was not rain water. When she felt between her legs, her hands were scarlet and she felt as if her belly was being ripped out. She knew what that meant—she had lost her baby. She lay there bleeding, retching and distraught. It was where they found her.

With the scourge of HIV/AIDS moving through the country at breakneck speed, a group of women from Malawi's capital, Lilongwe, had joined together to spread information about the disease. Some women worked in the cities, others regularly combed the countryside searching for victims to provide basic care, assistance and information. Perhaps it was destiny that drove this small group of compassionate women to find Chantal.

They washed her, cared for her using herbs and traditional medicines and provided basic first aid until the bleeding stopped and she could be moved. Two of the women remained with her and alternated with the others who climbed into their old mustard-colored bus and headed for settlements within a few hours drive. At first she could barely stand without fainting but within a few days she felt her strength return and with assistance she made it to the bus that had been leaving every morning and returning every evening since they had found her.

With everyone safely on board they headed northwest. Chantal was an avid listener and had always enjoyed a light-hearted conversation but this was no aimless chitchat. The women, totally committed to their project were only too happy to explain their mission in great detail. It had only been seven short years that Malawians could even speak about the disease. The government not unlike other African regimes had continued to stand fast that HIV/AIDS didn't exist in their country and any mention of the scourge was forbidden. Unfortunately during this time of denial AIDS had gained a tragic foothold in the continent's populations.

Chantal listened intently and poured over the literature she was handed but it wasn't until the creaky old bus pulled into her village that she came face to face with the devastation the plague was causing. The joy of meeting her mother and father and being home again paled when she saw familiar faces lying on pallets waiting for death to claim them. Children starving with distended bellies watched listlessly as the women lifted them, hugged them closely, fed them and drew their blood to be tested for HIV/AIDS. The hardest thing for Chantel was when a child would latch on to her hand and tell her that his or her "Mum and Dad were gone forever an' ever."

Chantal thought of how she felt back in Blantyre. There she considered her life complete and perfect. Now she realized that her world would never be complete or perfect, she was without a husband and without the baby that she had longer for. In spite of a feeling of total uselessness, or perhaps because of it, she asked the bus women to teach her their basic medical skills. With the crash course she learned how to administer to those who were victims of night sweats, tremors and chills, how to recognize cholera and malaria sufferers and how to draw blood and have it ready to be transported to Blantyre for AIDS testing. The following day the women left for Zomba, their last stop on this trip before heading back to their headquarters in Blantyre.

When the women returned with fresh supplies a few weeks later they saw a world of difference in the little village. Sadly there were fresh graves on a hillside, but those too ill to leave their huts were clean and their quarters tidy. Chantal had taken a few rusty tools to try to salvage the small plots of ground and the cleared fields gave evidence of some planting. Since the village's well, such as it was, had gone dry, the irregular visit of the water truck was a special joy. Chantal saw to it that it's precious cargo was equally disbursed and divided into drinking and cooking to bathing and clothes washing. In the evenings Chantel provided AIDS awareness information a subject that few wanted to hear about or discuss but that would change.

Her days were never idle. Her parents and the older villagers remembered her as the "tall little girl with the strong will" and they did her biding. The younger members soon lost their fear of admitting they were HIV positive and listened to her advice. But it was the little children she enjoyed the most. She was followed everywhere as she went on her self-appointed rounds and she could feel the children's eyes peering at her even when she had her back turned. When she went into the huts to administer to those barely alive she knew that her little shadows were at the doorway. And when she worked in the field they peeked at her from behind an unkempt goat pen. Eventually a few of the older ones found enough nerve to come closer to her and one morning two little boys grabbed her hand and held it for a few precious moments before scurrying away.

And so Chantal's life now had a new meaning. She awoke many mornings to the cry of a sick child. She cleaned the desolate huts and put together a makeshift first aid office in one of the shelters that had been vacant since the inhabitants made their way to Zomba in search of jobs and food. She watched for the signs of the bus women and delighted in the information, medicines and food that they brought. No matter how busy she was the children knew she would stop and run with them to the village entrance when the rasping old bus appeared out of a cloud of dust dancing across the flat lands.

At time went on Chantal was filled with a deeper sense of fulfillment that she'd ever known. Occasionally she'd leave the village for a few days to help the bus women make their rounds to another sun-bleached settlement. They never knew how bad it would be when they entered the stifling huts, some with only one small window, others with no windows at all. When Chantal returned to her village she delighted in the cheers and the warmth of the children and the old alike. She knew she had made a small difference in her village and it gave her a deep sense of pride.

However there are all too few successes, a baby here and there being saved by a wet nurse from the city. All too few blood samples coming back marked "negative" and all too few farmers who have a packet of precious seeds to plant. The situation is grim and she and the bus women feel as if the whole country is sinking into a dark sea of despair. So much of the population is mired in a hand-to-mouth existence, there is never enough medicine and the AIDS death rate is climbing leaving thousands of children orphans. As disheartened as they are it seems that there is always one in the group that has the where-with-all to bolster their spirits with a "tomorrow will be better." Knowing that there is little hope that any tomorrow in the near future will be better they go on with their work endeavoring to force a cheerful smile to those who have little to smile about.

Recently they've heard that news of the country's famine is darting across the world and that some countries are responding to their plight. They revel in the news and hope that the aid won't be too little too late. Chantal has come a long way, the women have come a long way. In spite of, or perhaps because of the complexity of their own day-to-day lives they continue to push ahead and deal with their nation's problems from a gender perspective and thus they are proving it is possible to fashion our globe into a better place.

Chapter Three

"Women have always been the guardians of wisdom and humanity which makes them natural, but unusually secret rulers. The time has come for them to rule openly, but together with and not against men."

—Charlotte Wolf

Tawanna's eyes swept across the tiny room. She didn't need the alarm this morning she'd been wide-awake most of the night. This day was going to be special—a climax to weeks of waiting. She churned over in her mind once again what she needed to do before heading for Lagos to visit her sister, Meena. Drop her son Jacob off at school and repeat instructions to the nurse-companion who she'd hired for Kudirat, her mother.

Ah, her mother. A slight frown crossed Tawanna's face as she thought of her mother. It certainly hadn't been easy attempting to pull her into the 21st century. Kudirat was mentally back to what life had been for generations and was steadfast in her resistance to change. Tawanna tried to stay tolerant but at times it was difficult to remain unruffled at Kudirat's daily outbursts of frustration.

"Why do I have to go with you to the hospital—it's too big. Why do I need to see a doctor? We did fine with Medicine Men. How can you sleep inside a building? We did fine in our huts or under the stars. Why do you need a 'wash machine?' We did fine using rocks at the lake. Why does Jacob go to school in a big building—boys did fine at our little village school. Why does he need to write? Just because you went to school and learned to write doesn't mean everybody else has to."

Questions, questions, never ending questions that always ended with Kudirat clucking her tongue disapprovingly. Perhaps she would never accept this new life in Nigeria's capital, Abuja. But her discontented murmuring only made Tawanna more resolute than ever. The life she'd carved out for herself and her son was the right life—the best life for her mother. The old woman was getting frail. Her leathery face seemed tighter, her gray-white hair thinner, her gait slower and her breathing labored. Still Tawanna couldn't help but chuckle to herself, in spite of it all the old glorious woman had the same vinegary tongue that Tawanna remembered from childhood. Their village would always hold a special place in Tawanna's heart. She could close her eyes and still see it dazzling in the sun with its maze of paths weaving between the mud huts and the small plots growing cassava, potatoes and root vegetables. With nothing to compare it to, the inhabitants continued to believe that their village afforded them a reasonably pleasant life. Had it not been Tawanna and her sister's fascination with learning, they no doubt would have spent their entire lives there. But in a country where only half of the women are literate, she and her sister had caught the eye of a local politician and friend of their tribal chief father who saw early on that the two girls had potential which meant moving to a bigger world. The two sisters left for school in Abuja where Tawanna eventually met her future husband, Ibrahim. Their life together had been good, they had produced a son all the while studying at the university and working in government offices until Ibrahim's life had been cut short by a bullet during an attempted coup in 1992. Meena had moved to Lagos where she was tirelessly dedicated to political and social issues and now she was pushing Tawanna to pick up the gauntlet and do the same at Abuja.

By the time Tawanna reached the train station the sun was already hot in the bright blue sky. Ignoring the stares of those who frowned on a woman traveling alone, she struggled to climb the steps of the crowded and stuffy train as it was beginning to inch away from the station. It seemed as if her life was full of struggles. Sandwiched between caring for Kudirat, keeping a watchful eye on Jacob and overseeing his education, she maintained her job and career and kept current on the country's many problems.

Nigeria seemed to be moving ahead and then it would stumble. In spite of the end of army rule and a new constitution in 1999, the country was still without a budget and mired in substandard housing, high interest rates, inadequate education and a meager job market, especially for women. AIDS education was woefully lacking which was causing all of Africa's life expectancy rates to drop. Poverty remained entrenched after years and years of military misrule and lawlessness was rising. Nigeria, Africa's most populous country was having trouble feeding its people, many of them going to bed every night suffering severe hunger pains and with little hope of finding enough food to meet their daily needs anytime in the future. The swaying of the train was almost blissfully hypnotic and by the time she noticed Lagos' buildings fast approaching and she caught a glimpse of her sister on the platform, Tawanna had lost her sinking feeling of hopelessness.

The two sisters talked well into the night. Meena was full of information. She spoke of the eight female legislators who had journeyed to the United States in May 2000 to learn about the political process and how to inaugurate citizen activism. Meena's eyes had a special fire when she talked of the enthusiasm sweeping through Lagos. More women were becoming active in politics, working together encouraging, organizing and demanding upgraded village schools improved roads, small cottage hospitals, electricity and clean water.

The red sun was peeking over the horizon as the sisters drank their last glass of palm wine. For as long as they could remember they had enjoyed the sunrises. It seemed as if the sky was always filled with mellow shades of orange and red and the village always quiet except for a few skinny goats scampering around their pen. The night had been fruitful. The goals and methods had been discussed, argued over and finally agreed on. Tawanna was still debating if she should launch her crusade with the women of the capital's surrounding villages or start off big with Abuja's women, but whatever path she chose she knew she was hooked. Her determination was furthered when they traveled through the Niger Delta's poverty-stricken villages. She thought of Jacob's healthy little body when she saw the children's swollen bellies and her heart ached when she met their parents some with little or no energy to forge for food for themselves or their children.

But it isn't just Nigeria's wobbling democracy that's in trouble—the whole African continent is in pain. Such a contrast to the multinational oil companies up-to-date equipment as they extract the country's valuable oil and send it off in tankers to supply the industrial countries' insatiable appetite for petroleum as they have done since 1950 when oil was first discovered in the region.

Within a few days Tawanna was heading home armed with posters, signs and folders stuffed with information. As the train edged from the station, she leaned back and enjoyed the sublime feeling of confidence she had gained. She as well as Meena would work to awaken and organize the women and she was confident that together they would be successful in improving their country. It was late at night when Tawanna tired and weary reached the apartment. Jacob barely stirred when she checked on him and Kudirat was sound asleep which was good, Tawanna didn't have the energy to deal with her mother, that could wait until morning.

For the next few months Tawanna worked tirelessly speaking to university women and female government workers. Organized into groups they studied and discussed the country's American style constitution and how to make their political figures more responsible to the people. Kudirat said little when Tawanna returned later and later in the evenings. Some nights she was enthusiastic, the meetings had been encouraging, the women were beginning to understand that they had power if they worked together. Yet other evenings she was distraught listening to other women comfortably locked in their traditional mindset accepting the denigration of women as it was now and always had been. Tawanna knew her mother wasn't concerned with what was going on but some nights she just had to vent to somebody and so she rambled on about her successes and failures. Kudirat with the utmost indifference said nothing and fixed her stare at her hands, the wall, the floor or out the window giving little indication that she was even listening. When the room finally fell silent, they'd go to bed with barely a word between them.

Days blended into weeks and weeks into months and Tawanna continued to work tirelessly. She met with women, she talked to women, and she cajoled the women. Finally she reached the point where she felt confident that she'd made inroads in organizing the various groups and molding their thinking about what female empowerment would mean to them. She'd watched the women bond during the months and she caught the overall feeling of affection and support that was developing between them. She figured that the city women would have fewer problems reaching the minds and hearts of the better-educated city people and she opted to spend her efforts reaching out to the villages surrounding Abuja and beyond. She'd schedule one little village at a time and perhaps word of her visits would eventually proceed her and make her task easier.

Her enthusiasm was catching. All of them were upbeat during their one last long meeting before setting out on their mission. It would take weeks, perhaps months, but their goal was to comb the capital and reach every woman, encouraging them to learn about the political process. The women left with an overall sense of passion, they were about to make that all-important first step to strengthen their fledgling democracy. In the spirit of the moment, Tawanna decided against taking the bus home. The dense clouds were cooling the air and the walk would help her unwind. Perhaps being more optimistic than she should have been, she made her way down the narrow streets, deep in thought and unaware that she was being followed.

Cutting across a park near the center of the city a large burly figure made his move. The chain of events happened so rapidly that Tawanna was unable to completely relive the incident for the police. All she remembered was being knocked to the ground and a dark figure tearing at her clothes. When she kicked him he reached for his knife and she felt a sharp piercing pain in her left leg. He held the bloody knife to her face and growled.

"Don't scream or I'll slit your throat."

For a split second she remembered how she and Ibrahim had made love so tenderly, so lovingly and now she was being taken in violence. He finally left and she laid there for what seemed hours feeling the blood flooding from the jagged gash in her leg. Her body was wracked with pain and she was too exhausted, too humiliated and too terrorized to try to get up. She felt her enthusiasm, her hopes for the future slipping away, the lawlessness of the country had finally caught up with her and she began sobbing. Two men out for a late night stroll found her, bloody and incoherent.

She remembered them carrying her to a car before she passed out. When she awakened she was at the Abuja hospital and a nurse and doctor were bending over her leg. She felt removed from reality. Everything and everybody seemed to be in slow motion. She caught a glimpse of the clock on the wall but the numbers were out of focus. She slipped into a comfortable daze but not before catching bits and pieces of strange sounding conversations floating around her. "Stitches . . . deep gash . . . loss of blood . . . save the leg."

Finally she escaped into a dark, safe and peaceful place with no pain or cares. There she watched Meena, a happy child running after the goats. Through the mist she saw Kudirat cooking and stirring her favorite thick pepper soup. Through the mist she saw the praise singers in their colorful turbans and finery. Through the mist she saw her father in his tribal dress holding court with the villagers. During the next few days she felt herself floating in and out of reality with no sense of up or down. Nurses always seemed to be hovering around her and she soon learned to expect frequent visits from one of the staff doctors, Dr. Davon Adedeji. When the delirium finally disappeared he told her that he and another doctor were the ones who had discovered her in the park. Only once did he touch on the subject of rape. Because sections of the country were still under the influence of Islamic law as they saw it, women were subject to death by stoning for any sexual activity no matter how gruesome and even though it was the woman who was the victim. To alleviate any further trouble, Tawanna's files indicated she was in hospital care because she had suffered a serious leg wound and no one ever spoke of the rape again.

Finally Tawanna was well enough to be driven home by a member of the hospital staff. Slow and unsteady she hobbled toward the apartment on crutches, every step an effort. The front door of the apartment opened onto a sea of well wishers. Kudirat and Jacob were there, the city women she had worked with were there and villagers who had made the long tedious journey to the city were there. It was a tiring day but a happy one and when she bid the last visitor goodbye she fell into bed exhausted. She awoke only once and found Kudirat's arms holding her. Her mother and her were drawing closer than they had in years. But in some ways the closeness wasn't enough.

Tawanna was sinking into malaise. It would be weeks, maybe months before she'd feel her energy return and be able to venture out to the country's isolated settlements. On especially dark days she wondered if she could ever recapture her dedication to become involved in the various women's causes.

The once high energy Tawanna was now content to loll in bed with a strange, fixed stare toward the window. Kudirat's amulets hadn't worked, her herbs and ancient concoctions hadn't worked and all she could do was watch her daughter deteriorate mentally and physically. When women from the university came by they quickly sized up the situation and left immediately for the hospital and Dr. Adedeji. He arrived at the apartment a few hours later.

To Tawanna it seemed as if he talked on and on. Her leg although still weak was healing, the infection was gone, she needed to get out of bed and put some weight on it so the muscles wouldn't atrophy. He repeated over and over that lying in bed wasn't helping her physically or mentally. She only halfheartedly listened, she wanted to be angry with him, to scream at him, but she couldn't. She just wanted him to go away. He didn't go away and his visits took on a persistent pattern. She became familiar with his knock most evenings after dinner.

As time passed Tawanna looked forward to seeing him and not just for his medical advice. His soft brown eyes and strong chin seemed to sweep through her and his visits lasted longer and longer. They talked of the past and their hopes for the future of Nigeria. One particularly lengthy evening she sat in the darkness mulling over his last sentence before he disappeared into the night, "the country needs more women like you."

She spent the rest of the night thinking and realizing that to stop now would be to devalue all she had accomplished. She opened her books and papers and spent hours reading and rereading them. Within a few weeks even though she still felt twinges of pain in her leg, she created an agenda and picked the first site she planned to visit. She couldn't have known what astonishing twists of fate lay ahead.

Some of the city's outlying enclaves were nothing more than dismal shantytowns. Many Nigerians eager for a better life had moved off the land and headed for the cities. In essence they had swapped one wretched state for another. Their shacks were composed of cardboard, tin or anything else they could scrounge from trash heaps. Children were malnourished and listless. Older boys with their fathers searched endlessly for work. The young girls had little to occupy themselves save the care of a toddler sister or brother. The women usually had a baby at their breast, all of them seeped in a culture of scarcity.

Tawanna began explaining her visit as the crowd gathered. At first they feigned interest but as she continued to speak about good government they nodded to each other knowingly about all the past promises the government had made and had kept none of them and slowly, ever so slowly they'd drift away.

The weeks went on, the visits went on across the tormented land. For the most part Tawanna was barely tolerated until Dr. Adedeji and Kudirat accompanied her. The doctor brought medicine and advice, being careful never to overstep the group's medicine man or his spiritual trinkets. Kudirat, extremely reluctant at first, finally came along much to Tawanna's shock (and her pleasure). While her mother was limited in her scope of experiences and didn't understand much of what Tawanna was preaching, she eventually realized that whatever was going on it meant a lot to her daughter. Kudirat's presence added a feeling of camaraderie to the meetings when it became known that she'd lived most of her life in a settlement not too terribly unlike theirs.

It seemed the farther and farther they reached into the countryside, the worse conditions became. The isolated villagers had to forage farther and farther away for wood, which meant that miles and miles of land had been denuded. Meager crops, the result of sparse rainfall meant less food to be shared. In many instances a precious drum of water was used for drinking, cooking and washing dishes. While they may not have been satisfied with what they had, they didn't know what was on the outside, and sadly some didn't care to know. Tawanna realized that it would take many visits and time to move them past their preconceptions of their lot in life.

All was not lost however. News of Tawanna's crusade eventually darted across the landscape. As her reputation grew so did the crowds, full of questions. When would they have local elections, why had the elections been postponed again, and when would the politicians honor their promises? Much of the time the questions would be flung into the air at a rapid pace allowing little time for answers. Tawanna, always casting an optimistic eye to the future, told of her dream where city women and countrywomen were informed, organized and joined together to walk shoulder to shoulder during demonstrations for better conditions. She provided information on the New Partnership for Africa's Development with their own President Obasanjo along with similar officials from South Africa, Senegal and Algeria who had committed their country to "good governance and respect for human rights."

Her passion and enthusiasm was evident when she talked about the group of women who had held a major oil company at bay by a non-violent occupation of an oil flow station in Makarabe. The women, successful in keeping the station idle for eleven days the summer of 2002 had presented Chevron with a list of demands, not the least of which was clean water, electricity and a cottage medical clinic to meet their needs. And she spoke of a future when the black gold would afford their country the riches and assets it desperately needed. Few of the audiences already knew that their country continued to be Africa's largest oil exporter.

Democracy was inching across the continent, albeit slowly but it was moving. Tawanna always caught their attention when she spoke of other nations such as Sierra Leone, a nation not unlike theirs who had suffered through a bitter ten-year civil war and yet had the political machine in place to cast ballots for a new president in May 2002. Some in the audience perked up when she spoke of

Lesotho whose voters had gone to the polls in spring 2002 to elect a new Parliament. She could hear the whispering and catch the smiles when a few women nudged each other and spoke of relatives living in Lesotho. The listeners were always interested in photos and Tawanna displayed pictures of women in Mali standing in line with babies on their backs or at their breasts waiting patiently to vote. Many times their meetings would draw to a close with Tawanna, almost overcome with emotion as her eyes searched the audience for a sign, any sign that the women were listening and fired up.

"If these countries and more can move toward good government why not Nigeria?"

More often than not women caught her fire and boisterous cheers would rise from the crowds at her last sentence.

"We can do it, all of us joining together in a sisterhood. We are the most populous African nation let's make everybody know that we are moving ahead."

Tawanna would then mumble under her breath, "for the alternative is too depressing to even contemplate."

Eventually Tawanna and her entourage would visit all thirty-six Nigerian states sometimes crisscrossing the southern part of the country only a few days after Meena. Both sisters remain unwavering in their work against the force of tradition, endeavoring to alter women's sense of who they are and to be cognizant of the cultural restraints that had forced them to take a subordinate role.

But for Tawanna, all is not just work in her life. The evening arrived that would be the best moment, in the best week, of the best month of her life when she and Dr. Davon Adedeji would make a commitment to each other. Thus Jacob has a new father and Kudirat a new son-in-law. Dr. Adedeji is diligently working to get used to Kudirat's vinegary tongue, which probably is a good thing, her sayings and beliefs keeps him on his toes and at times, chuckling.

While they all can look back at what they have accomplished, breaking down the barriers and bringing together women of different ages, of different areas of the country, of different spiritual beliefs, urging them to remain informed and take an interest in their government, none are disillusioned, least of all Tawanna. She realizes it will take time for the country to overcome the many years of military dictatorships and forge ahead to its rightful place in the world economy. As time passes there will be subtle and not so subtle changes some with radical implications on women's lives but that is all in the future. For now she is content to revel in the unity and warmth of the city groups and similar groups in the countryside. All of them are slowly and steadily moving ahead and being empowered. The future may not look as bright as they'd want but at least many of them have a new outlook on their role in life and know that they can accomplish many improvements when they unite not only for their sisters but for their nation at large.

Chapter Four

"When self-respect takes its rightful place in the psyche of woman, she will not allow herself to be manipulated by anyone."

—Indira Mahindra

Melina slammed the phone down for the third time since breakfast. Just when she thought her life was in order she'd heard from her mother in Crete. Just when she thought she had no obligations to her family she was ordered home. And just when she vowed she'd never go back, she found herself pouring over ferry schedules with trembling hands. After the third phone call it seemed as if all the progress she'd made to forget the past was for nothing. Her family was reaching across the watery miles and creeping into her life again. On the verge of tears she wondered if she'd ever be free of them, was there no place they couldn't reach her? Wasn't the span between Athens and Iraklion, Crete's largest city and her childhood home large enough?

Ah, her childhood—it was anything but happy and peaceful. From the moment she was born her parents made no effort to hide their profound disappointment that she wasn't the first-born son they had hoped for. Her mother sank into depression because she was convinced she'd failed her husband. Making the most of the situation her husband took advantage of his wife's melancholy by engaging in philandering with several local young women. The following year when his wife became pregnant again and had a miscarriage, it was Melina who had "brought bad luck to the house." This thinking continued through the years even though three sons, Otho, Nicos and Cyrus had been added to the family. While many families in Greece discounted the presence of daughters and afforded their sons every advantage, Melina's parents seemed to take the custom to a new level. Whether it was a failed business venture or a relative's health problem, they were convinced Melina harbored the Mati, the 'Evil Eye' and thus were responsible. As the years passed Melina was barely acknowledged at home. In school she devoted herself to her studies. Accolades from her teachers went unnoticed and even though she had been awarded an ample scholarship to continue her education she was discouraged from accepting. Any extra money for travel and books would go to her brothers. Thus she found herself unappreciated, unloved and alone with no one to pour out her feelings to, until a new priest, Father Darius, arrived at the local church and befriended her.

One might wonder if it was destiny that had reached out and pulled them together. Darius was a restless and handsome young priest, tall and broad shouldered, with deep-set brown eyes and the beginning of a dark beard. He had a certain magnetism and dominated any gathering he attended. The sight of him in his elegant red and gold liturgical robes at services caught many a young woman's eye. The Archbishop, sensing Darius' restlessness, had transferred the young man from a small church on the northern side of the island to the larger one in Iraklion. Actually Darius had an uneasy alliance with the church. At the same time he was questioning his own vocation he was also involved in an attempt to impress his superiors with ideas to increase young adult attendance at religious functions. Melina who had little else to occupy her life after family chores attended church functions even when some of the others ignored them. Soon Darius and Melina's few words of greeting underneath the long wall of icons at the back of the church had grown into long conversations.

The 'dates' were harmless at first. There were meetings at the marble Renaissance fountain, Ta Leontaria, near the city's open air market crammed full of colorful fresh fruits, assorted vegetables and delightfully vibrant flowers that had been loaded onto wagons and trucks from country gardens before the first rays of the morning sun. Many evenings found the young couple sitting on a comfortable rock, eyeing the harbor's traffic and talking about anything and everything. Within a few short weeks both realized that there was something more that each of them wanted from the relationship and it wasn't long before they were living for the moments they would be together.

Darius longed to hold Melina, to have her in his arms and tell her she was important to him. Melina, in the blush of first love was ecstatic; at last someone cared for her. As their passions rose their dates took on an air of secrecy and long drives to isolated beaches and lofty palm groves became a mainstay of their lives. One afternoon as the last of the sun's rays was dropping behind the horizon Melina lost her virginity. She was convinced that the next step would be marriage and the thought of fleeing her family's home and starting a new life set her heart racing. As she lay in Darius' arms she wondered if life could get any better than this.

The following month Melina was unwavering in the belief that Darius would greet her news with great joy and her eyes were brimming with anticipation as the evening unfolded before her. She attended vespers, pretended to mouth the prayers and waited impatiently until the last person slipped out behind the heavy oak door. All alone now, she headed for the alcove off the sanctuary. Perhaps it was fitting that the discussion they had was near the sanctuary. Voices were never raised there, only muffled tones of people seeking advice, a blessing or a prayer. Screams were never heard there, it was a holy place, a place of peace. With a bright smile and a happy heart she told Darius of her pregnancy. At first she couldn't believe what he was saying.

Darius removed his priestly garments painstakingly slow and deliberate. Finally almost in a rasping whisper he spoke of his life being stuck at a crossroads. Perhaps he'd leave the church, maybe soon, maybe later. Further, he was in a quandary as to the career he'd follow. On a grimmer note he was emphatic that whatever the future held for him it didn't include a baby and marriage. Melina stood trembling, she was sure she could feel the blood draining from her face. She wanted to scream, to cry hysterically but all that could wait until she'd left the sanctuary.

Outside in the pitch black heavy night air she sobbed and screamed as if her heart would break. An hour earlier she'd felt so elated, now she was completely crushed. The old feelings of being totally alone were pushing the very breath out of her. She must have walked for miles up and down various streets teetering on the edge of time and event and care. Unfortunately the evening was not over yet. When she arrived back at her house all hell was about to break lose. The neighborhood gossips, those empty people with little else to do beside carrying tales from one house to another, had taken enormous delight in the fact that it was their duty to see that Melina's parents were fully aware of what was going on between their daughter and Father Darius. Indeed they had been seen together on a beach and they were doing more than just enjoying the sea and sun.

*   *   *

Had it only been two years since she'd hastily flung a few clothes into an overnight case, grabbed her moneybag from under her bed and cowered in her room until the uproar and clamor ceased before tiptoeing carefully out of the house? She remembered the wild dash to the port to catch the last ferry of the evening for Athens. Safely aboard she never looked back. Months later when she recounted that night she realized how much of a chance she had taken. She had no place to go in the huge city. She was pregnant, frightened and totally alone with her family's words throbbing in her ears. Not aware of their daughter's pregnancy, they concentrated on the fact that she'd been seen "with a holy man." She had been "a temptress to a man of God." And worst of all, "she'd disgraced the family and they all would have to pay for her sins." Actually the truth was different, very different but Melina knew her parents would never believe that.

The past two years living in Athens had been so peaceful and pleasant. After being accepted at a convent whose main mission was housing and comforting girls in the various stages of their pregnancies, Melina bunked with another young woman, Irene, a successful psychology teacher at the famed Athens University, who longed to get back to the classroom. They soon became friends and after each of them delivered healthy baby girls they left the convent together and found an apartment where they shared their determination to create a new life for themselves and their babies.

As time went on and before their money completely ran out they found jobs, a reliable baby sitter and began to enjoy the hustle and bustle of Athens. While Irene was happy teaching she was still hopeful that her married lover, another university professor, would leave his wife for her and her baby. Melina had no such hopes for herself. In a weak moment Melina called her family in Crete. Maybe, she reasoned, her mother would forget the past and be happy for her. Alas, it was just a daydream, and a bad one at that. The call was anything but pleasant. She never got a word in and after listening to her mother's sobbing and her father's cursing about being "a temptress" she sadly clicked the receiver and the conversation, if one could call it that, was over, finished. It was several moments later as Melina dried her tears that she realized that she hadn't shared her news about her precious little girl, Diana. As she watched her baby sleeping peaceful in the pale pink baby basket next to her bed she vowed she'd never contact her family again. It was a vow she wouldn't be able to keep. While she may have been able to somewhat loosen her strong ties to her family, deep inside she struggled with deep emotional scars. On a happier note, to the outside world she appeared a striking and self-assured young woman.

She was tall and stately with well-formed legs and body. Her complexion was flawless, the hint of pink on her cheeks and her full red lips were made more noticeable by her shimmering coal black hair she wore neatly in a bun at the nape of her neck. She was the epitome of glamour in her dark blue suit and crisp white blouse that signaled she was an employee of OlympiaAir. She was well liked by her coworkers and devoted herself to her job, which landed her two promotions in a year.

How could she have known when she awoke this morning that this day would be vastly different from what had gone before? She bathed, fed and dressed Diana before depositing her at the baby sitters in an apartment on a lower floor of their building. With a hug and a wave she left for what she believed would be a pleasant and busy day at the office. She had no idea that the cocoon of safety around herself that she had labored so long and so hard on was about to be shattered by her mother's stinging decree to come home "for a special event." No amount of begging off because of work reached her mother who was engaged in her usual ranting. The pattern was the same, mother and father ranting, daughter hanging up.

Melina felt the walls of her small office crowding in on her and squeezing the very breath out of her. Before the telephone buzzed again, as she knew it would, she made a hasty exit to the building's bright and sunny open center court filled with the gentle scent of jasmine, basil and lavender. Huge pots of cascading bold splashes of bougainvillea stood near the oversized and soothing fountain where the employees often ate lunch, smoked and flirted. She found a bench under the shade of a stately old cypress tree and tried to collect her thoughts. Why had her mother called her after so many months, and why was she so insistent that she come home? While Melina was becoming more anxious by the minute she took solace in the fact that they didn't know about Diana. That very fact led to a serious discussion later that evening with Irene.

"You go home just for a day or two Melina. Take little Diana with you—just to show her off."

"I can't, I just can't."

"Well, you can't keep her invisible forever."

Melina knew Irene was right, someday they'd know they had a granddaughter but for now she wanted her baby safe and away from the fray. As the ferry eased out of Piraeus, Athens's main port, she wondered what she'd find at the end of her journey. Actually what she'd find there would frighten her beyond her wildest dreams. Melina burrowed down in her seat and took inventory of the other passengers. She envied the young men and women no doubt with little else on their minds except how to enjoy a fun-filled weekend at the island's busy bars and clubs or discovering Crete's many pleasant beaches. She watched the lighthearted children moving within sight of their mother's watchful eyes, laughing and giggling while playing games with their older siblings and new friends. And her eyes rested on travelers about her parents' age holding hands and seemingly content with their lives and their memories of many years together. With a sigh she wondered if she would ever find that special someone to share her life with. The gentle hum of the engine and the sway of the waves caused her to drift off to sleep until she felt the bump of the ferry as it inched into Iraklion, one of Crete's main ports.

On dry land Melina was greeted by her Aunt Theodora and little cousin, Toula who Melina remembered never seemed to smile. Her serious dark eyes, short straight black hair and a constant frown gave the child a somber demeanor. It was a few minutes before Melina realized that Toula had not taken her eyes off of her. When the little girl opened her mouth her question was bold and direct.

"Melina, what's a virgin?"

No one spoke. The scene was made more uncomfortable when Theodora yanked Toula around and smacked her hard on her behind. Between tears the little girl continued.

"But Moma, everybody says she's not a virgin . . . she'll burn in hell someday. And what about that priest guy . . . Huh?"

The three of them continued their walk in stunned silence. At the house Melina was greeted awkwardly by her parents and brothers and given a sharp once-over. Everyone appeared to be in a hurry to have the meeting over with and get on with his or her activities. Melina was barely seated when her father backed up by her mother began to speak. Their paternal grandmother recovering from a serious hip fracture was soon to be released from a hospital and could no longer live alone. Melina thought, well, so far so good. This doesn't concern me. Then the bombshell was dropped.

"Melina, we're prepared to pardon you for what you did to Father Darius . . . you know . . . tempting him and all." All eyes that had been searching the floor were now positioned on Melina as her mother full of moral indignation continued.

"Now . . . of course, YOU have to ask for our forgiveness."

Melina's father chimed in. "We all see eye to eye on this. We'll try and forgive you for what you did."

Melina's mother's glance darted from one to another as they nodded in agreement.

"I think we all feel that we'll try to let the past go. You are to leave Athens . . . come home . . . we need you to take care of your grandmother in her final days . . . she's going to need constant care."

Feeling a certain pride that the family was so gracious to their prodigal daughter, she stopped talking and stared at her hands. The gears in Melina's brain finally clicked into place. Her heart was beating so loudly she wondered if they could hear it across the room. While still in a state of shock she found her voice and summoned all the self-control she had.

"I'm to ask your forgiveness? All my life you've acted as if I didn't exist and now I'm to ask YOUR forgiveness?"

"You don't know what you're saying. You're just tired." Her mother stood up and gave one more command.

"Go up to your old room and get ready for the party to celebrate your moving back in with us. We have invited everyone we know."

Melina was relieved to escape the highly charged room at least for a few minutes. Upstairs she slowly inched open the door and came face to face with the bedroom she had spent so many unhappy hours in. It was eerie. Her tattered dolls, her books, her clothes, and even her nightgown folded across the bottom of her bed were the same as when she'd left. She felt as if she was in a time warp. A quiet knock on the door brought her back to reality. It was her favorite brother, Cyrus with a troubled look on his face.

"Melina, hey, they're convinced you're coming back here to live." His voice dropped almost to a whisper and his eyes were intense. "Listen to me. I've heard them talking . . . they're planning on making you stay."

"I'm not staying."

"Well your best bet is to get the hell out of here on the first ferry in the morning."

Sister and brother sat on the bed and talked of the games they'd played when he was a boy. Teasing good-humoredly he laughed, "I knew I didn't always win Melina, I knew that you were always told to let me win."

A half-smile crossed her brother's face as he added, "Hey, guess what? I'm getting married this summer to a great gal. You know what Mother asked me when I told her? She didn't ask if Barbara and I got along, if we were in love, if Barbara was pretty, where we'd live . . . hell nothing. All she asked—'is your fiancee a virgin?' Ah, you know how she is, Melina . . . then she jumped into the same old tirade we've all heard hundreds of times of how you tempted Father Darius. Melina ignored that last statement and took a deep breath.

"Cyrus, neither one of them will ever get over the past. You know what living here would be like for me?" She didn't wait for an answer. "It would be a living hell. Well, I'm not coming back here to live or to even visit . . . ever. I shouldn't have come back now. I have a new life and am happy in Athens."

She hesitated for a moment. Should she tell her brother about Diana? No, she decided at least for now, she'd keep her secret. Cyrus left and Melina lay on her bed and stared at the ceiling. Suddenly she felt very vulnerable and turned her face into the pillow to hide her tears before heading to the fray downstairs. The house was quickly filling up with guests. A long table reaching from the kitchen through the dining room and into the parlor was heaped with food. Melina was ordered to cut and serve small cubes of roasted lamb and slices of onion flavored with marjoram and garlic. Large bowls of yogurt with cucumber, garlic and squid sat at both ends of the table amid ample bottles of ouzo and wine. Side tables were laden with koulouri, delicious bread rings with sesame seeds. Trays of dolmades, those tasty rolls of rice and meat wrapped in vine leaves were passed around and the trays were refilled as soon as they were empty. As the evening wore on the family's bouzouki was brought out and everyone danced to the music of the mandolin.

Melina forced herself to smile all the while she was vowing to herself that if she heard one more person congratulate her for seeing the error of her ways and glad she was coming back home to live she'd scream. She did hear another person and operating on pure adrenaline she did scream. The music stopped, the laughing stopped, the gossip stopped, the drinking stopped and even the chewing stopped. The house fell silent which only made the tck tck tck of the wide old mantle clock seem louder than ever.

"Hear me out! I'm only here for tonight. I'm living in Athens and that's where I'm staying."

With that Melina dashed out of the room. She knew that the ferry wouldn't leave for hours but she would rather endure the heavy rainstorm that was blowing across the island than remain at the house. By the time she got to the terminal she was soaking wet and cold. The hours passed slowly, the rain ended slowly and the sun made an appearance slowly. As the port came awake she boarded the first ferry of the day. Safely on board and heading north to Athens she found a seat off by herself and closed her eyes. Was the night only a bad dream? Had all of it really happened? She shivered and longed to feel safe again in her apartment with her baby in her arms.

Irene stared at the woman in the doorway with disheveled hair, damp clothes and tear-stained face and wondered if the person was really Melina. Irene helped the wet traveler get into dry clothes and into bed where she laid down beside little Diana and held her close. It was then that Melina recounted the nightmare she'd been through in Crete. The exhausted young woman finally drifted off to sleep clutching Diana's small pink hand. Irene tiptoed out of the room while pondering if Melina would ever be able to fully rise above all of her damaging family experiences.

Life for the two mothers soon returned to normal at least on the surface. Off in the morning to jobs, home at night to be with their little daughters. A weekend day at the main open-air market was a special treat for the children as well as their mothers. There were frequent trips to the National Gardens where they enjoyed the sun and the scenery. While on the surface Melina appeared to be in good spirits it was those times when she drifted into silence and seemed to be reliving old hurts that worried Irene the most.

Melina would never fully understand why on that particular day, at that particular hour she did it. Later she would wonder, could it have been destiny that prompted her to make a stop on her way home? She passed the ornate breath-taking Cathedral of Athens and entered her favorite little church next door, the Panayia Gorgoepikoos, dedicated to the Virgin Who Answers Prayers Quickly. She'd always felt at home in its smallness and quietness. The delicate aroma of incense blended with the fragrance of numerous flickering amber candles and gave the main altar a serene effect. Melina lost herself in prayer and was so deeply transfixed she was oblivious to the movement of another person in the sanctuary. When she lifted her eyes, her heart almost stopped. As she watched the tall man in priestly garb their eyes met in a moment of recognition. No mistake about it, it was Darius.

While the rest of the evening was almost a complete blur she would re-member following Father Darius to a little side garden where they awkwardly stood before each other and attempted to engage in a light-hearted conversa-tion. Finally Darius got to the serious events of his life. He looked calmly into Melina's eyes and told of being transferred to Athens a few months after she'd left Crete. Yes, he had decided to remain a member of the clergy and as time went on he was pleased with his decision. And as if it was an after thought he added, "By the way, can you believe it? I'm married now and very happy." Melina felt her stomach clench as she told him of Diana and while she wasn't sure what reaction she expected—it definitely wasn't the one she heard.

She searched Darius' face for a clue to what he was thinking. At first his face was maddeningly blank. Then almost in a panic he asked.

"You're not going to make a fuss about this are you? You know go to the Archbishop?"

When Melina shook her head no, he gathered his wits and continued.

"You must be a wonderful mother, I'm sure you'll raise a wonderful daugh-ter." And as if to ease his mind further he added, "You're sure . . . you're sure . . . you're not going to make a fuss about this? You know my reputation and all . . . and another thing, my wife wouldn't understand . . . She's pretty closed-minded about this sort of thing."

Melina left and entered the cooling night air. She could've taken the bus home but decided to walk to clear her head. Thoughts of her affair with Dar-ius tumbled through her mind. Scenes of her mother, of her family bounced around her in rapid succession. By the time she climbed the long steps to the apartment she realized it wouldn't be easy but she had to put all of it behind her, but how? Perhaps Irene would be the key.

It began slowly at first and almost without notice-Irene giving a helping hand to a young woman lugging a contrary stroller with a wobbly wheel up the stairs in their apartment complex. As they exchanged pleasantries it was hard to ignore the lines of frustration drifting across the young mother's face. The image stayed with Irene and gave form and purpose to her dream of bringing women together, who for whatever reasons were raising their sons and daughters alone.

The one-night-a-week-sessions began meagerly at first with just three women relishing the camaraderie but within six weeks Melina and Irene's apartment was filled to capacity with chatting women eager to share their hopes and their dreams for themselves and for their children. The meetings became a harmonious haven where the members could confidentially bring their problems and choose to speak or not, of emotional entanglements that were suffocating them. Melina was able to overcome the estrangement from her family that haunted her and it was a red-letter day when she finally washed out of her very heart and soul the feeling that she was to blame for her parents' actions and beliefs. She had suffered too long from misplaced guilt for disappointing them in their hopes for a first son. Now she realized they would have to deal with their problems themselves, she was proud to be a woman and she resolved never to let them take that from her. Longer in coming was Melina's triumph over the insecurity that resulted from the mistake she'd made falling headlong into a relationship with Father Darius, the result of which pushed her to mistrust all men.

After several months it became evident to Melina and Irene that the group had outgrown their small apartment. Fortunately because of the favorable publicity the group had, a conference room on the first floor was made available to them and it is here that they continue to meet. They are an exotic collage of dedicated women assisting a 'sister' working through the trouble spots of life whether it is a serious illness, separation and/or divorce, facing a difficult pregnancy alone or dealing with an unwieldy child. It is not uncommon to hear a hesitant knock on the door and an unfamiliar face apprehensively hoping to be invited in. Whatever she might need she will, no doubt find it here.

They have come a long way from the first meeting. They have a name now, "Athena's Women." News of job openings, a dress shop with an end-of-the month sale and recipes are exchanged and enjoyed. Baby sitting for a shopping spree or a night on the town is always available and excursions to the beaches or to the city's special performances of the opera and symphony are events they share. Engagements, weddings and the birth of a child are celebrated with gusto. And speaking of weddings, Irene has moved to a larger apartment with her new husband. He is a highly acclaimed member of the Athens symphony and Irene has learned to enjoy violin music. Melina is seeing a professor from the University of Athens and they speak of a happy future together raising Diana.

The journey of life includes many triumphs and sorrows, many of them overpowering but these female movers and shakers have learned to reach out to each other to solve critical issues and thus all women gain. Their example to their sisters causes them to take pride in their gender while challenging the status quo.

Chapter Five

"From a timid, shy girl I had become a woman of resolute character, who could no longer be frightened by the struggle with troubles."

—Anna Dostoevsky

Elga had already awake when the sun's first rays cut into the bedroom. She had listened to the wind storming most of the night and shortly before dawn the longed-for cooling rains began to pound the casita's white walls. During this time of year rain was always welcome—summers never changed—they were unbearably hot. Today was going to be special. After weeks of exasperating negotiations she finally had acquired an old multicolored school bus that was destined to get her and her husband, Luis, and their villages' handicrafts to Guatemala City.

The sound of Luis tinkering with the bus engine reminded Elga that it was almost time to leave. She dressed quickly while rehashing the long chain of events that had brought them to this day. She remembered the sultry afternoon when word about her brother, Jorge, reached the village. He'd been one of the countless young men searching for adventure and thought he'd found it fighting in the civil war that had ravaged the country for years. The message read that Jorge had been wounded and was in one of the capital's hospitals.

Elga couldn't forget the look of despair on her parents' faces. Her brother had been their pride and joy. They didn't care on what side he'd fought. Their happiness was evident during his sporadic visits when they listened intently to his accounts of faraway places, tales of ambushes, victories and defeats, surviving in caves and living off the land. More than once Elga watched the villagers standing in awe aching to touch his gun as he swaggered about with it slung over his shoulder. To appease her parents, she knew what she had to

38

do. They wouldn't be content until her brother was back with them so she took on the task of finding Jorge and encouraging him to return home. How could she have known that the trip would change all their lives forever?

Many times when she thought about the long journey she also remembered how her feet and legs had throbbed with pain due to the endless walking. And she couldn't help but shiver when she recalled wadding in chest high water following the all too frequent torrential rains. She wondered if the poor old lame donkey she had rode after bartering with some bandits was still alive. She tried not to remember the uncomfortable sensation of bouncing over the isolated and rutted roads in dilapidated buses and trucks and the sharing of space with pigs and chickens heading to market. What a relief it was that day to see Guatemala City rising in the distance.

It would always be etched in her mind how she felt when she finally found Jorge. Once his muscular legs had been pillars of strength as he lugged loads of firewood and fruit on his back working for wealthy landowners a half-day walk from the village. Now his legs were gone the result of a land-mine explosion and he was lying in bed removed from reality by a constant supply of painkillers.

Elga had never strayed far from home. She'd been content to remain confined to the women's traditional role of being a good wife to her husband, raising children and taking care of her parents. Perhaps that was why she was so caught up in the excitement and exhilaration of the big city. When she first arrived she lingered at Jorge's bedside night and day and under the watchful eye of the floor nurse, Connie, she learned to change his bandages and when he sank into agonizing pain she held him in her arms, calming and comforting him.

But as time passed Elga began to feel the energy of the city reaching out to her and overwhelming her senses. More and more she found herself wandering through the crowded colorful markets, studying the people, admiring their clothes, following a few steps behind as they strolled down the narrow streets stopping in a shop that had caught their eye and emerging with bags stuffed with jewelry, native costumes and a host of souvenirs. Compared to her little sleepy hamlet it was if a whole new world had opened up to her and it sent her heart racing. The very items she had in her home were being (to her) sold at unheard of prices.

Tourism was fast becoming Guatemala's second industry after coffee exports due to the government and the rebels signing the Peace Accords in 1996. To everyone's relief a semblance of peace seemed to filter through the country especially in the major cities. Tourists meant shoppers—loads of shoppers with loads of money eager to gobble up native crafts, the very crafts that the country's craftsmen had traded and bartered among themselves for countless centuries.

Elga reflected on that fateful day when she returned to the hospital and found Connie wheeling some of the amputees out on the somewhat cooler veranda, one of the staff's daily chores to help the patients cope with the hot, stuffy hospital wards. The two women found a comfortable spot under an old oak tree and at the risk of her feeling that she was on the verge of doing something seriously foolhardy, Elga unfolded her plan. Connie, always anxious for a diversion, was more than happy to listen.

They mulled over the problems, rejoiced uneasily at the perceived rewards and whenever she seemed to slip back into doubt, Connie was always there reassuring her.

"You can do it—I know you can and I'll help you."

This was precisely the encouragement that Elga needed. They hugged and agreed that Elga should leave as quickly as possible to set the plan in motion. The return journey was made somewhat easier by riding with one of Connie's relatives heading home after selling and bartering his crops at the city's huge downtown open bazaar. He was able to drop her off about fifteen miles from her village.

Elga used the long walk home to plan, plot and polish her strategy. It was then that she decided nobody needed to know that Jorge's legs were gone, that he was only a shell of a man they had once known. Instead she'd announce that he was fine, he was working, he had a beautiful house and had plenty of money.

Elga sighed as she made her way toward the bus. In spite of all her well-laid plans, it hadn't been easy encouraging the villagers to hand over their traditional homemade colorful cloth, sculptured wood figurines, woven mats, herbs and anything else that she suggested. Even though she had spent most of her life with them in the remote settlement many gave a deaf ear to her crusade to bring change to the sleepy little village that hadn't changed in generations. At times she was exasperated listening to the same endless comments drifting from the thatched huts or coming from the women milling about around the outdoor kitchens. They were eking out a living they reasoned. They had little interest in crowded cities filled with foreigners. Still she tried, coaxing, pleading and cajoling.

Some days were particularly tense. Some of the villagers avoided her entirely; others looked past her no longer listening. But eventually she discovered that all was not lost. A tiny spark of interest was brewing among a few of the women who had spent many evenings by themselves in the bushes discussing her proposed venture. Possibly she was right they reasoned. Perhaps her idea would bring them money and maybe their children could go to a real school and escape the menial jobs that once had been their fate. The more they talked the faster they talked and their enthusiasm spread like wildfire.

What one woman didn't say another one did. They were tired of barely getting by, tired of seeing their husbands and sons working for a pittance clearing land, digging roads, building foot bridges far enough away that they were absent from home for weeks at a time. That was all Elga wanted to hear. She no longer was alone in her dreams of a better life!

After endless hours spent jamming the bus with the villagers' contributions, Luis primed the engine and they slowly edged away from the village. Elga turned and glanced once more at the group waving good-by, some faces happy and hopeful, others with eyes full of apprehension and still others feigning disinterest, convinced that the venture wouldn't gain anybody anything. But that was all right, she decided. She'd show them.

While Luis was not as optimistic as Elga, he was eager to visit Jorge and listen to his exploits. Elga knew she'd have to explain her brother's medical condition to Luis eventually but it could wait until they were beyond turning back. She realized that her husband had only agreed to her idea because he felt that Jorge would take over the entire operation. Elga was bent on a mission that she was sure would afford money for her and her husband and she was ready to do anything to see that it happened.

The rickety old bus carried them past denuded forests, across unsteady bridges and fields ablaze with wildflowers of yellow and red. Elga and Luis talked little. It was difficult to carry on a conversation above the din of the engine. By evening as the sun left the cloudless sky Luis stopped the bus near a peaceful stream. It would turn out to be anything but a tranquil oasis.

They found a spot under a massive shade tree and when Elga felt Luis' arm reaching across her shoulders they drew closer. In the spirit of the moment, she began a bit guardedly to talk about Jorge's condition. At first the silence was deafening then Luis screamed and she saw the burning stare of his eyes as he jumped to his feet.

"You tricked me."

No amount of her trying to explain the situation helped, his ears were deaf to anything she said and she felt her face bearing the brunt of his anger and his fists. Blood trickled from her nose and her left eye was completely shut. She fell to the ground and his boots hammered into her back. When he searched his pockets for a knife she caught him off guard and made a dash for the bus and slammed the door. The next few hours were agony. Elga's face was swollen and bleeding, her body was wracked with pain and she lay sobbing on the hard floor. Luis continued his rant as he circled the bus and beat on the door. Before dawn they both had dozed off and for a short time each had a respite from the violence.

The sun was barely making an appearance when Luis armed with a heavy rock broke a window and climbed in. Elga cowered under one of the seats fearing a repeat of the previous evening. Luis spoke in a cold monotone and his eyes were blazing.

"You bitch, tricking your husband . . . you say we'll make money . . . well, you'd better be right." He took a long, deep breath before shrieking, "Get this, you bitch, that money's going to be mine . . . all mine . . . this'll teach you to trick your husband."

For years she'd remember every detail of sight and smell and sound of that night. He had beaten her before when he returned to the village drunk after jobs had dried up in the north but the previous night had been the worst. Ever since they'd been married she rationalized that the violence was just part of their daily lives, it ebbed and flowed through their casita, through her parents' casita and throughout the village, a reaction to stressful events, perceived wrongs and fears of a loss of dominance.

Luis gunned the engine and soon the bus roared onto the road. Elga's satisfaction was muted, they were still heading toward the capital but she was in a limbo of anxiety. What lay ahead for them now? At the outskirts of Guatemala City the bus lurched to a stop and while Luis fiddled with the engine's carburetor Elga found a cool stream and washed the blood from her face but she couldn't hide the bruises.

They finally pulled into the dimly lit hospital parking lot just as Connie was about to begin her night shift. She stared at Elga, aghast at her appearance. With little time to talk she quickly directed them to the supply room where two discarded mattresses awaited them and they dragged the lumpy and stained pads to an isolated patch of grass on the hospital's sprawling grounds. Although smarting from her injuries, Elga was exhausted and fell into an uneasy sleep. She awoke even before the sun made an appearance and found Connie towering over her, eager for answers.

"What happened to make you look like this?" Elga turned away from Connie but she would not be dissuaded. "Answer me! How did you get those bruises?" Connie gave no indication that she'd stop and she had no intention of leaving without Elga. "Get up! You're coming with me into the hospital."

When she noticed Elga glancing over to Luis' empty mattress several feet away she mumbled sarcastically, "he left during the night and good riddance."

On their way to the wards Elga made excuses. She shouldn't have kept the truth to herself. She knew Luis never liked to be pushed into a situation. It was all her fault he got angry. Luis was a good man. When he got over it, he'd come back and that would be the end of it. Connie listened in eerie silence but a few feet from the entrance she exploded.

"This isn't your fault, can't you see, he's a bastard." Elga turned away. "Listen to me, you don't have to take this."

In the second floor restroom Elga glanced at the image in the mirror and gasped. Her face never had looked so bad. She sobbed inconsolably. All her plans were unraveling. Jorge had taken a turn for the worse and was barely alive connected to a morphine drip. How could she bring back that news to her parents? And now Luis was gone and she didn't know when he'd come back and forgive her.

Elga moved inside and bunked with Connie in the hospital's sparse employee quarters. While her cuts and abrasions were healing she sat at a window and frantically watched the main highway off in the distance hoping for sign of Luis and the tattered old bus with its precious cargo. Finally one afternoon he did return and Elga, forgetting her injuries, rushed to meet him. She was full of questions but he wasn't in a talking mood. He stood in front of her rumpled and unshaven staring at her for what seemed an eternity. Then a sick grin swept across his face and he pulled a wad of bills from his back pocket.

"See this—it's mine—all mine.

No amount of pleading, no amount of begging would change his mind. He told her more than once that he didn't give a damn about her or the villagers and throwing his head back she heard a terrifying defiant laugh before he strutted away. Elga was distraught. When she entered the bus she felt as if her heart had stopped. Everything was gone, the colorful cloths, the sculptured wood figurines, the woven mats, even the herbs that she had cajoled the villagers to give her to sell.

Elga and Connie talked for hours. Well, that is Connie talked as Elga sat slipping every so slowly into a dark hole of depression as she pondered how her plan had gone so terribly awry. Connie gave her advice and made suggestions but Elga's ears were deaf to them. The days passed and in spite of all of Connie's pep talks Elga remained listless and buried under layers of guilt. Luis was gone most of the time now and more than once Connie had given her pat answer to the situation "he's gone and I say good riddance." It was easy for Connie, Elga decided. She had a job, she wasn't in love, she didn't have a dying brother and most of all she didn't have parents and villagers eagerly awaiting her return.

Just as Connie was feeling that all her talk had been wasted, Elga began to think about her limited choices. No matter what else lay ahead of her she knew she had to find a job and pay the villagers back. She had long since stopped hoping that Luis would reappear and forgive her and more and more that thought was less and less unsettling. Her ribs were healing. Her cuts and bruises were all but gone except for the ones not visible.

Sections of the city were devoted to manufacturing and trade and Elga landed a job at a coffee bean plant a short walk from the hospital. She guarded her paychecks, her little cache of money was growing and she figured she'd be ready to pay the villagers back in a few months. She couldn't have known what fate still had in store for her.

Tired after a lengthy day at work, Elga neared Connie's quarters. The two women rarely saw each other with their schedules. Many nights Connie worked ten hours and by the time her shift was over, Elga had already left for her job. When they did see each other Connie lost no time in counseling Elga about her life and her values. One evening as Elga headed home she caught sight of a familiar form sitting under a tree. For an instance her heart skipped a beat, it was Luis. He was too engrossed to notice Elga watching him as he put a small dirty straw to his nose and began sniffing white powder. Elga left the scene with a knot in her throat and unaware that she was being followed.

By the time she opened the door to Connie's quarters, Luis' was only a few steps behind her. He shoved Elga inside and slammed the door. As he sat down on the bed he began to speak in a strange rapid-fire pace. He wanted money. He missed her. He wanted money. He forgave her. He wanted money. He vacillated between ecstatic highs and muffled lows. One minute he was lighthearted and happy, urging her to forget the past and speaking about grandiose plans for their future together. The next minute he'd be crying that he didn't know where his life was going and she'd be off better off without him. But always the ranting returned to money. He needed it, and he knew she had some.

She would never be able to explain it either to herself or to anyone else. But then again some things are beyond explanation. After months of living with Connie and listening to her, Elga had found a sacred spot within herself, a place of peace and quiet and especially pride and she wasn't going to give up what she'd found. She spoke with a detached calmness.

"Yes, Luis I have my wages, but that money is for the villagers. All my money is going to them. You left me with nothing."

He couldn't believe what he was hearing. He could always talk her into forgetting his misdeeds before. He pleaded, he threatened, he tried to pull her body to his, his hands reaching for her breasts but she resisted. His anger mounted as he stormed through the room, searching drawers, smashing dishes to the floor, yanking clothes from the all-too-small closet, ripping the bedclothes off the bed and tearing open pillows, still he couldn't find the money.

Perhaps if he had noticed a small trap door in the floor covered by a tattered old rag rug, he'd been successful. Connie and Elga had hidden their money there in two small rusty old tin cans. More than once they lifted the floorboard and counted their cash just to give themselves a sense of security and well being. Elga fearing the worst ran to the door.

"If you don't leave I'm calling a guard, you'll be put in jail."

Still Luis lingered, cursing and threatening. A guard did come and the last Elga heard Luis was cooling his heels in jail. But things would get worse. Luis had tried to knife a guard. Now he was considered a long-timer and was removed to a high-security prison. Elga and he would never meet again. Still at times she'd think of him and ache for their lost love.

The day would come when Elga would return to the village. Connie had arranged for a dealer to drive her back so she could pay off the villagers and make plans for future sales. The long trip was unnerving. They were the same rutted roads, the same shaky bridges she had traveled across months earlier and yet they were different. Perhaps it was because she was different. Months earlier she had hopes and dreams for her marriage, her brother and her village. Now her marriage was over, her parents would soon have to deal with Jorge because the government was returning him to his home a broken man with two stumps where strong solid legs had once been. And while the villagers were happy with the money and the plans for future sales, they eyed her differently. She had been to the big city, she had a new life, she had moved out of their kinship group.

While Elga felt the pull of the village, she also felt the pull of the city. She spent hours rehashing all the rewards and the problems of a life away from all the familiar places she had known as a child but she knew what she had to do. Jorge was safely settled and their parents' lives would center on him but then again it had always been that way. Female children always took a back seat to a male child. After the initial shock of seeing Jorge's condition, their parents had resigned themselves to the sameness of his every day life, being carried to the village square, catching the sun's rays and enjoying the villagers' attention. He continued to live with the notion that his power lay in his gun and it was never far from his side.

Elga waited for the dealer to return from his jaunt through the countryside looking for items to sell to the rich foreigners. She'd ride with him back to the capitol. There was no fan fair this time when she left, no one waving goodbye, no one calling out "hurry back." She'd go back of course, bringing food and other items but she'd just as quickly return to the city.

Several months later, through the efforts of Connie, the hospital began regular workshops for battered women. Elga became an assistant in this endeavor and spoke openly about the abuses she had suffered. She encouraged the women to talk about their marriage and helped many come face to face with the fact that their union was fraught with enmity and battles for control. The road ahead for some women will be difficult, some even view abuse as some sort of affection and they continue to accept the cycle of violence. Others find it difficult to leave the social confines of a male dominated and sometimes violent society. Still others are living with failed dreams while others never have had any dreams and they are the hardest to reach because they ac-cept the hopelessness of their lives.

The classes continue to be a mainstay of the hospital for it is where most females acquire a sense of self-esteem and find the courage to carve out new lives. Connie and Elga labor tirelessly and pray that their encouragement will spill over from the mothers to their daughters and each generation's females will no longer accept the subordinate role and someday, someday the cycle of domestic violence will stop.

Chapter Six

"Keep away from people who try to belittle your ambitions. Small people always do that, but the really great make you feel that you, too, can become great.

— Mark Twain

Nona tried to ignore the dull sound of the dirt as it hit the casket sinking slower and slower from sight. She took a deep breath and let her eyes dart across the small gathering of friends and relatives maneuvering umbrellas against the penetrating cold and rainy weather. There were others there too, the same familiar faces that always seemed to show up at a burial near the outskirts of Cork City's oldest and largest cemetery. In spite of the occasion Nona felt buoyant and contented. They'd done all the traditional Irish things, the flowers, the wake, the rosary and the funeral mass just as Ol' Granny wanted. Now it was all over, the chapter was closed.

The small circle of relatives and friends offered their proper condolences and began to drift slowly towards their cars. Nona stared at the procession of vehicles moving along the curving road before climbing a steep hill and disappearing into the horizon. She wondered what the mourners would do this afternoon. Stop at a pub, perhaps make a visit to their parish church or chapel or maybe ring up a friend or neighbor to gossip and exchange views on the morning's funeral. Well, whatever they did she didn't care, she had the rest of her life all planned out and it made her heart beat excitedly. Suddenly the sound of shrill weeping caught her attention.

Mike, her husband of over twenty-seven years, could no longer hold back the tears. Nona wanted to be sympathetic but she was no stranger to the sound of his crying. It was the same cry she'd heard numerous times following a session when his fists pounded her face and body and then tag after her to beg forgiveness. And it was the same cry she'd heard through the years the morning after a drunk when the house was in shambles with broken furniture and a few smashed dishes for good measure.

She inched away from Mike and out of earshot of his sobbing to move along the graves pretending to read the headstones or to admire a special statue on top of a grave. The rain was coming down heavy now and she made a dash for the protection and warmth of the car. She mulled over the best time to tell Mike that now was her time. Lord knows she'd put it off long enough. The first time she brought up the subject she'd watched in horror as Mike slammed his fist on a table toppling a crystal lamp and screamed.

"We're just married you can't do that right now. There's no money. Anyway what do you know about that kinda stuff?"

And so she held her dreams in her heart for later. By the time their daughter Maggie was ready for preschool she approached the subject again and the reply was repeated.

"You can't do that now; you have a daughter who needs you at home. Do as I say and forget it."

When their son Liam was born the message had become a well-used refrain.

"I want these kids out of school before you do anything like that. Anyway, that crazy scheme will end you up in the poor house."

Well, "the kids" were adults now. Claire was in Dublin writing her thesis for her expected doctorate in history. Liam was living and working in England at *The London Times*. Just when Nona felt the time was ripe for her she heard the same worn phrase from Mike.

"Forget that damn idea, my Mum needs you at home."

And so Nona quietly put her plans on hold again but she never forgot them. She poured over decorating publications, scavenged recipe books from flea markets and old book stores for miles around, made cost analysis, studied profit and loss statements and most of all spent hours talking to Ol' Granny about her ideas. Now her dream would finally be realized! She was going to open her very own tearoom in the heart of Cork City.

Ol' Granny considered Nona special, actually more special than her own children, who seldom made any effort to call, write or visit her. In fact it had been years since Ol' Granny had seen any of them. One afternoon after the frail old woman awoke from her nap she tapped her cane on the floor to signal Nona in the kitchen downstairs that she was awake and needed her. Nona put an extra log on the fire to ward off the early evening chill before she climbed the stairs. She figured Ol' Granny wanted to be lifted out of bed to her favorite old chair by the window to watch the street happenings as she did every evening and Nona made a mental note to get the soft old shawl from the hall closet and wrap her in it. But Ol' Granny didn't want to be moved, not just yet.

She motioned Nona down on her knees and indicated that something out of the ordinary was under her bed. Nona reached an old decrepit wooden box with rusty hinges and the veneer curling on its sides. She had noticed it when Ol' Granny first came to live with them but put it out of her mind as something that was dear to the old woman and none of her business. They opened the box and between pieces of the disintegrating dark blue velvet lining came face-to-face with a thick wad of paper money and a handful of rare coins.

"Here Dearie, it'll help you get your tearoom."

Nona's eyes widened when she saw what she thought were the old woman's life savings.

"I can't take this from you, what will Mike and your other kids think?"

"You have been a good daughter-in-law; I want you to have it. And indeed I don't give a damn what anybody thinks, especially Mike." Then the old woman winked at her and softened her voice almost to a whisper.

"Just let it be our secret. And Lass, follow your dream and don't let anyone get in the way, not anyone."

Nona replaced the box under the bed as the old woman's words took on an air of mystery.

"There are some other things in the bottom of that box that you might find very interesting when I'm gone."

To say that Nona was excited would be an understatement. She thought of the wonderful cache of money all the time as she brought the old woman her meals, helped her to the bathroom, untangled and brushed her mane of snow-white hair, changed her sheets and fluffed her pillows. Thoughts of her new-found riches bounced around in her head before she fell asleep and were the first thing she thought of in the morning. It was comforting to know that more money had been added to her savings and that all was safe and sound in a soft white linen bag under her preserved old wedding gown in the attic. Mike would never find it there.

It wasn't easy for Nona to keep her exuberance hidden. She was constantly on edge in front of her husband and measured everything she said or did when he was home. More than once he asked why she was staring at him during dinner. She'd brush off his question lightly, fearing that her secret would gush out any minute but the thought was dancing around her head, "oh, if you only knew what's in the attic."

The next few weeks Nona watched as Ol' Granny's condition worsened. The doctor came and went and said her heart was about to give out. Father Harrison came and went and prayed for her soul. Nona tried to be pleasant to him but there were too many things between them. The dark night she fled to the rectory to escape Mike's drunken violence was burnt in her mind. At first Father Harrison had been comforting as he listened to her story. Mike was drunk again. Mike had broken some of the kitchen chairs and Mike had beaten her when she refused to cook dinner for him. But when she told the priest that she was leaving her husband and filing for divorce all his compassion vanished.

"Woman, you know you can't leave him. He needs you. A wife's place is with her husband, you know that. And get that nonsense out of your mind. There's no divorce allowed in the church. You just have to pray more."

"Pray more? I'm tired of praying for Mike. I'm tired of praying for our marriage. I'm always praying and where does it get me?

"Don't talk like that. Prayer works wonders. I'm ordering you to go to confession and receive absolution for these evil thoughts. Perhaps you've had too great an expectation of marriage."

She listened and could hear the thump of her heart beating as she felt the anger rising and almost choking her. She wanted to scream an obscenity or two at him but instead she bounced to her feet, buttoned her coat and reached for the doorknob. His last remark had little comfort in it.

"When I have time I'll go and have a little talk with Mike. Ah everything will work out you'll see."

Well, everything did seem to work out for a few short weeks but eventually all hell broke lose again. Late one Sunday evening aware of what was happening downstairs, Ol' Granny used all her energy to scream and curse Mike but it didn't help. Nona watched with tears streaming down her face as Maggie and Liam hurriedly packed their belongings and left home for good. There had been no love between them and their father for they remembered all too well his behavior through the years. Nona was proud of her children, they'd escaped their home and made new lives for themselves and someday she'd do the same. This thought sustained her even as she sat in church and listened to Father Harrison preach on the blessings of the family. She watched his eyes scanning the pews and resting on her when he admonished, "wives be subject to your husbands."

No one could ever accuse Nona of being impatient. Indeed one could question her judgment to remain year after year after year in her rocky predicament. But she had been raised in the way of an old Irish custom which had remained unmodified through each generation and had as one of its mottoes, "be patient—there is nothing to do but wait." She wasn't aware of it then but she was a victim of her culture, walled in by domesticity, religion and societal expectations. It would be no small task to break out but she made the first step on a damp drizzly morning a week after Ol' Granny's funeral. After breakfast, as she had done for years, she packed Mike's lunch in the same old dented black metal lunch bucket and bid him good-bye as he left for his work at one of the city's famed breweries. Now the only sound in the house was the gentle tick-tack of the old mantel clock in the parlor and she reveled in the peace and quiet. Upstairs she reached under the bed and pulled out Ol' Granny's box. What she saw inside pulled at her heartstrings!

A folded-in-half large brown envelope with bold lettering, "Susie O' Malley's will" laid next to a small time-weathered leather diary with entries dating back to the old woman's marriage to her husband Tomas over seventy years ago. Nona didn't open the will; she figured Ol' Granny couldn't have much left to leave anyone. But curiosity got the best of her when she picked up the small diary and held it in her hand before opening it. The pages were dog-eared and the black ink was fading in places but enough was left to speak volumes. Nona pulled Ol' Granny's shawl closer and sat on the floor and unhurriedly began to turn the pages one by one.

"I'm so happy. This was my wedding day. Oh, how I love Tomas. I'm praying that I will be a good wife. I hope I give Tomas plenty of babies."

A tear came to Nona's eyes as she remembered her own wedding day and all the hopes and dreams she had for her own marriage to Mike. Not wishing to dwell on that subject for any length of time she took a deep breath and thumbed through the pages to some four years later.

"Tomas doesn't seem to be happy. He wants to go and fight the British. I told him he couldn't that he had to take care of me and the babies. I think he was going to hit me even though I'm in the family way again. Tomas is not happy."

Several pages appeared to have tea stains running down them and the letters were barely legible.

"It's spring again. The babies have bad colds from the long hard winter. Tomas hates to hear them cry. He left this morning and didn't say when he would be back. When I went looking for him my heart fell. I saw it with my own eyes. He was laughing and walking arm and arm with that bitch Bridget down near the market."

A few pages later revealed more of Tomas' philandering with other women.

"Tonight I peeked in the window of Brown's Pub. There he was, in a booth cuddling and feeling the teats of that street-walker Susie Smith. Doesn't he care about me and the kids anymore?"

A later entry read, "I think the whole damn town knows that Tomas is the father of Bridget's baby. At church the women look at me funny. They are so smug as if their own husbands are angels."

Nona's heart went out to Ol' Granny. She could almost feel the rage reaching out and grabbing her from the pages as the old woman mentioned her next step.

"I can't stand it any longer. I'm going to face Tomas tonight and tell him of the gossip and what I know, the bastard. At first I cried because he had broken my heart, now God forgive me, I hate him. I hope he burns in hell someday. Oh, God, I should be ashamed to say such things."

Nona couldn't put the book down. "Father Meyer came today. I told him about Tom. He said I had to pray more. I have no place to go anyway."

The following page laid bare a story not unlike Nona's.

"My face is healing pretty well—my eyes are still black and blue and they hurt a lot. Tomas was angry I talked to Father Meyer. The children saw him beating me."

A later account was especially poignant. "Oh, God, I've cried all day. I'm in the family way again. God forgive me but I don't want any more kids, this'll be my ninth. I'm so tired all the time and Tomas doesn't give a damn. I must be a wicked woman not to want more children. I'll pray to the Virgin Mary to forgive me."

Nona dried her eyes and laid the diary back in the box. She felt as if she had entered an mystical place—a sacred place—the old woman was speaking to her from the grave. How terrible a life she'd had, trapped in a loveless marriage with young children some no more than a year apart and no place to go. Now she understood why their talks always seemed to end with Ol' Granny, her deep blue eyes intense, encouraging her to "make your own way in life." As a tribute to the old woman she was going to do exactly that and do it now.

She caught a bus and was lost in thought as it rolled downtown. She'd had her eye on a vacant store for months and it figured strongly in her dream to have her own tea room. The location was good, it was in a busy part of the downtown area near the Southern Channel and the River Lee and with the perfect sign out front she'd be a success, she just knew it. The real estate agent, Paula Greely, a happy-go-lucky plump woman with short gray hair and a quick smile was an easy person to talk to and very helpful. They chatted most of the afternoon as they paced back and forth imagining the front room filled with elegant mid-size round tables and imitation velvet green chairs. The somewhat narrow entry was just the right size for some tall lush plants either side of a podium where the greeter would stand. A back room was spacious with many shelves to hold baking and other supplies. Everything else was fine, except the kitchen.

The room was definitely a problem. The cupboards with lopsided shelves desperately needed a few coats of varnish, the sink was scratched and cracked and the overhead lights too plain and too dull. The refrigerator had lost its shelves and the ovens lacked control knobs. At Paula's urging the absentee landlord, a rich old gentleman who had made most of his money in Dublin real estate and glad to have a new tenant, agreed to Nona's demands. Soon workman were coming and going and the kitchen came alive with new lighting, an extra large refrigerator and freezer and repaired ovens. The cabinets were refinished and new sinks installed. For the next month Nona spent her days scrubbing and polishing and planning.

A chimney sweep took on the fireplace and left hours later covered with soot. The cracked and peeling paint in the tea room was sanded until smooth and disappeared under fresh soft mint green enamel. Luxurious dark green carpet was laid and the colorful stained glass light fixtures that hung from the ceilings gave off a soft warm glow. Tables and chairs arrived and the tea room took on a cozy atmosphere. A trompe l'oeil expert did wonders with the walls. Windows appeared where they hadn't been and opened to beautiful green fields with yellow and blue wild flowers. A tall grandfather clock came alive on one wall with its hands stuck on twelve noon and was banked with huge baskets of red roses. Nona couldn't remember when she'd been so contented.

Paula dropped in on her almost every morning to eye the improvements and chat over a cup of tea. On Nona's way home one evening she realized that Paula knew more about her plans than did her own husband. She would have to tell Mike tonight after dinner. Yes, that was it. Everything would be out in the open. She couldn't have known then that there would be some very harsh painful bends in the road ahead of her.

They ate in silence. The only sound was the click of the knives and forks against the plates and the crackle and swizzle of a new log in the fireplace. Finishing their last cups of tea and before Mike put on his heavy parka to head for the neighborhood pub Nona spoke.

"Mike, now that Ol' Granny's gone, well, I'm going to open my own tea room."

"Like hell you are. Why in hell do you keep harping on that for? I've told you over and over that you won't make a go of it. Stick with what you know, do the wash and keep the house clean. I see now that you should've had more babies.

Nona realized that this wasn't the time or place to mention that it was Mike's fault that their family hadn't been larger. Instead she took a bold step in a different direction.

"Mike, I've already started work on a small shop and I'm not turning back."

Before he had time to digest what she said Nona continued to reveal what had been happening during the past weeks. She watched Mike's face go from an ashen gray to a fiery red and then his hand shot out and she sensed a stinging blow to her face. Over and over she felt his heavy fist. When she collapsed to the floor he put both of his knees on her arms and pounded her into unconsciousness. She didn't know how long she'd laid there but when she came to, the house was empty and cold. She spent the rest of the night putting warm packs on her face and slept little. Before the first blush of the day Mike shook her to get up to fix breakfast and pack his lunch. There were no words between them and neither looked at each other. Nona was relieved when he reached for his coat and muffler. Half-way out the door he hesitated for a brief second and mumbled, "By God I'm still the boss around here." With the slam of the door she had the warmth and peace of the house all to herself. Oh, how she wanted to crawl back into bed but she had an appointment to meet some suppliers at noon and she struggled to get dressed. The mirror wasn't kind and she did her best to camouflage her bruised face with cosmetics.

Paula was already lingering outside the shop when Nona got off the bus. She was aghast at Nona's unsightly face. With a sudden urge to talk and with no one else to confide in Nona laid bare the ugliness of her marriage. They chatted in the kitchen for what seemed hours as they tried to get comfortable on some empty wooden crates. Could the church help? No, she'd already tried that. Could she rent a small apartment? No, all her money was in the tea room. Then Paula suddenly jumped up.

"I've got it! What about the back room? Hey, there's space back there for a mattress. Then when you build up a good trade you can find a real apartment, what do you think?"

Nona had to admit that it was an a pretty good thought. She rolled it over in her mind for a few minutes and then her spirits rallied.

"Yeah, I guess I could do that. I'll go home one more time and get my clothes."

"You can't go back there. It's too risky. After you're finished with the suppliers call me. I'll drive you home and wait for you." Putting her arm around Nona, Paula added confidently, "I'll get you out of there safe and sound, you'll see."

Fighting the early evening traffic and the wet, slick streets the two women finally reached Nona's house. When she put the key in the lock and opened the front door neither woman could believe their eyes. Drawers lay open, spilling out their contents. Tables were overturned, closets appeared in disarray and every room was in shambles. She could hear Mike's stomping about as he shrieked at her to come upstairs.

"Have you seen Ol' Granny's will? I've looked everywhere, even in the goddamn attic. Listen here Lassie, if you think you're going to get any of my Mum's money you'll crazy. Tomorrow you'll get your comeuppance. We have an appointment with Mr. Fleming, the solicitor."

When Mike mentioned the attic Nona looked at Paula and put her hand over her mouth as if to stop a scream. Thoughts were tumbling over and over in her mind. But wait, maybe Mike hadn't looked at everything in the attic. But what if he had? He never mentioned finding any money. But what if he was just being cagey? If only she could nonchalantly go up there and see what had been disturbed. She swallowed and tried hard to control her voice.

"Why did you look in the attic?"

"Aw hell. I remembered an old wooden box with some of her things in it and I thought it was up there."

"I think that box is under Ol' Granny's bed. Did you look there?"

Mike fled to the bedroom, grabbed the box and tore the lid off. When he opened the envelope he roared.

"You got her to change her will, didn't you? Look here."

He waved the will back and forth near her face but fast enough that she couldn't read it.

"Well, we'll see about this tomorrow. You'll never get away with it."

Nona remained silent lest any remark from her would lead to violence. Paula was standing between the kitchen cupboards and tried to melt into the wall. Thankfully Mike never did see her. When he left for the pub he still was ranting and raving. Nona's eyes followed him down the street and when he no longer was in sight she dashed up to the attic. What a relief! Her wedding dress box hadn't been disturbed. She reached in and found the linen money-bag, then packed her clothes and Paula and her left for the tea room. After a sleepless night on a lumpy old mattress she dressed and prepared for the visit to the solicitor.

Nona slowly trod the few blocks to Mr. Fleming's office. She noticed that many of the flowers in the window boxes outside the small businesses were drooping under the weight of the heavy morning dew. Their condition made Nona think of how droopy she felt. And when she heard the church tolling its bells for early mass she said a silent prayer that all would go well this morning. She just wasn't up to handling any trouble from Mike today.

Across town Mr. Fleming was speeding to his appointment and damning the third green light he'd missed in a row. He was still fuming over his wife's overdrawn checking account, his unwed daughter's baby teething and crying all night, his secretary who had notified him she was ill and wouldn't be in for a few days. He hoped that all would go well this morning. He just wasn't up to handling any trouble from Mike O'Malley today.

The meeting opened quietly enough. Everyone was in their assigned places. Mr. Fleming sat at a main desk, flanked on either side by the two wit-nesses who had been present at the signing of Ol' Granny's will. Nona and Mike ignored each other and sat on a bench facing the trio. Mr. Fleming opened with the required legal information, yes, the will was legal and bind-ing and any legal action in an attempt to break it would be "superfluous and ill-advised." For several years Ol' Granny's bank account was added to regularly by "her deceased husband's ample railroad pension."

"This amount in full is to go to my daughter-in-law Nona O'Malley.

This revelation caused a furious outburst from Mike but was quickly squashed by Mr. Fleming's cold stare and swift nod to a guard who placed himself behind Mike.

"The land and the old farm house is also to go to Nona O'Malley as a small token of my appreciation for her loving and tender care of me in my last days."

A later codicil added, "The furniture and farm implements are to go to my children with Mike overseeing the distribution."

Mr. Fleming droned on and on with page after page of legal forms, which he shuffled, reshuffled, checked and rechecked. Finally signatures were called for and the session was over. Outside Nona felt as if she was walking on air as she headed back to the tearoom. She could hardly believe it. She had more now than she ever though she'd have. So lost in thought she was she didn't realize that a familiar form was following her on the other side of the street. Safely inside with her new found resources she paid some bills, ordered a new mattress and designed menus to provide the hoped-for patrons quite a bill of fare. Scones, various flavored baguettes, cinnamon tarts and new twists to Irish soda bread were offered along with the traditional Ploughman's Lunch, that most delicious thick wedge of cheese with various meats and condiments to be washed down with an assortment of teas. She then telephoned the Convent School to inquire about hiring some girls to help in the tearoom. The bake ovens were fired up day and night and everything seemed to be coming together. Opening day was around the corner!

What a day it was! The Mayor of Cork was present. The Chamber of Commerce sent a representative. The local listings magazine, *The List* ran a story about "Ol' Granny's TeaRoom" and locals and tourists filled the place. So busy Nona was she didn't have time to notice a figure lingering across the street for hours in a doorway of a vacant shop. The day finally ended with Paula helping her clean up. Nona realized she was happier than she'd ever been in her life and she knew sleep would be long in coming this night. After hugs and congratulations Paula left for home and was relieved that the figure of the man she had noticed earlier was gone from across the street.

Nona stretched out on her new comfortable mattress. Was all this really happening to her? It was something she had wanted for so long, yet at times she was filled with insecurities. What if Mike was right, she had "no right to do such a thing." What if nobody came? What if she ended deep in debt? The old familiar phrase that had been flung at her more times than she could count, that one phrase that could cause one to stop chasing their dreams, "you'll end up biting off more than you can chew" danced around in her head.

Nona realized that the first month was a test. Even though patrons came and went it would be the regulars who would decide if the tearoom was to their liking. Some days she made expenses, some days she was short. Other days she made a profit and was uplifted as she counted the day's receipts. She added new items to the menu and watched carefully to see if they should remain or be discarded. So busy was she that she never noticed a figure still lurking across the street many evenings as she locked up, doused the lights and headed for her mattress. But all that would soon change.

One evening just before she nodded off she could hear fumbling with the back door lock. Panic gripped her. Somebody was trying to get in. Grabbing the phone, the police were quick to answer her terror-stricken call. Within minutes with sirens blazing they had the intruder by the nape of his neck. Even in the dull light Nona recognized Mike.

"Lady, he says he's your husband. Are you guys separated? He wants to come in, is that all right with you?"

She didn't want to see him, hear him or be near him but he looked so pathetic standing by the policemen that she nodded "yes."

Nona and Mike spent the next hour chatting aimlessly. He was impressed with the tearoom as his eyes scanned the walls, the comfy table and chairs and the lush plants by the door. But Nona knew that there were more serious things to discuss and when Mike asked how much money she was making she ignored his question.

"Oh, by the way, I've talked with Father Harrison. He said I was right; it's my duty, my god-given duty to be head of the house. Nona don't you see, I have the right as your husband to tell you what to do."

Mike was pacing back and forth from one of the baking ovens to the refrigerator and back again as his eyes searched the floor.

"Of course," he added somewhat sheepishly, "if you are making money here, well I could go ahead and let you continue to operate the place. And another thing, you sleeping down here, that's not right. Come home with me."

Nona moved towards the door with her mobile phone in her hand. She was ready for anything.

"Mike it is over, finished for us. You won't change and I am not going to put myself in danger any more. I'm tired of going around with a swollen face, all black and blue. Just get out."

Mike let out a string of curses, she was a "wanton woman, a sinner, she'd loose her immortal soul" and on and on but he did leave. New locks were put on the doors the next morning and life continued as Nona wanted. When Father Harrison called one day to "help her to come to her senses" she barely listened to him. There were other things on her mind. Paula was up to something and it would bring joy to both of them.

It happened quite slowly at first, Paula bringing in a woman or two just for a chat and a cup of tea. Nona never knew where Paula found them, actually she never asked. But Paula seeing what Nona had gone through was now volunteering at one of the city's homeless shelters for women. Young girls, the thirty-something crowd, the middle aged and a few in their sixties or older were seen tagging along with Paula as she brought them to the tearoom and told them about her friend who had been down and out and yet had survived with grace and dignity. If she could do it, they could too.

Today Ol' Granny's TeaRoom is closed one Friday afternoon a month for that is where the women meet to encourage each other, to dream and to discuss how to make their lives better. Some women are in seemingly insurmountable situations with little skills and work experience and with young children and husbands or lovers or boyfriends quick to handle any stressful situation with violence. Nona has hired many of them and some are becoming quite proficient as they labor over the bake ovens.

In her private moments Nona "talks" to Ol' Granny and feels her presence. Their bond reaches across time and space. Nona is convinced that her old mentor knows about the tearoom and is pleased.

Nona has officially moved out of her house. Mike is pursuing a young woman he met at Brown's Pub and while he is "living in sin" it is Nona who is considered the one most lost, she has filed for divorce even though the church has condemned her actions. Her life is now just as she always wanted it to be. She gets great pleasure from her tearoom, but also from reaching out to those women who, for one reason or another, are down on their luck. Because of her inspiration they are dealing with their insecurities and taking a second look at their lives and some no longer accept violence as a part of a relationship. They are sisters connected to sisters and making life better for all of us.

Chapter Seven

"It is not in life but in art that self-fulfillment is to be found."

—George Woodcock

North Africa's hot winds were swirling across Sicily and sweeping through the bedroom window when Teresa turned in bed. The dust-laden sirocco was always with them this time of year, pushing hints of tan into the delicate Mediterranean blue sky. She'd linger this morning, no need to rush to work. Today was going to be special. Her working life was now behind her.

It hadn't been an easy decision leaving the massive old kitchen tucked behind the olive groves where she and so many of her friends and relatives had labored for countless years, sorting tender black and green olives before preparing them for international specialty markets. She'd miss the chatter, the gossip, the good-natured ribbing wandering in from the groves to blend with the chatter, the gossip, the good-natured ribbing that constantly bounced through the kitchen.

She had prayed. Oh, how she had prayed week after week fingering her rosary beads at Naso's Church of the Salvatore pleading for healing. When her husband, Antonio refused to journey with her to a grotto a half-day ride from home she remained undaunted and made the trip alone. She was convinced that the cave's healing waters would help her and she closed her ears to his comments.

"I'm not going and you're not going because the whole idea is just women's nonsense."

At first she was sure that the waters had helped. She felt stronger and she seemed to lose the stiffness and the swelling and some of the pain that had plagued her joints for years. But as time passed hauling the wooden baskets heaped high with olives through the various kitchen stations was becoming more and more difficult. At day's end it was becoming harder and harder to make her way to the company van for the evening's bumpy ride home.

Perhaps she'd worked long enough she reasoned. Perhaps it was time to be satisfied just shuffling around her hillside garden pruning, coaxing and picking its bright red tomatoes. If she became lonely she'd lazily stroll down to the town's square to linger with all the other women laughing and gossiping in the shade of the gnarled trees that had been planted centuries ago. But best of all she'd now have time to spend on her beloved artwork.

As far back as she could remember she'd found peace in her art. One of her pastel drawings was hanging in the Church of the Salvatore near the baptismal font for the entire town to see and another larger one was proudly displayed in the main dining room of a local convent. Even during her early birthing years when she could, she'd snatch a few precious minutes to devote to her artwork but as the family grew she found little time for her easel, charcoal and pastels. And of course, there was always Antonio commanding.

"You're to forget all that nonsense. Keep your mind on your housework and family."

Well, now she'd have the quiet of the house all to herself during the day as Antonio had announced loud and clear that he had no intention of retiring from the iron works where at age sixteen he had began his apprenticeship.

Teresa remembered when she'd first noticed Antonio and his big grin as he bragged about his work, fashioning candlesticks, intricate fireplace irons and small unique sculptures for the Naples market. All of the town's young girls were giving him the eye but he had settled on Teresa. Actually they were two of the few young people who hadn't had to endure an arranged marriage. They built a life together and produced eight children—seven of them sons and they were proud of every one of them.

Two boys had remained relatively close, living in Messina, laboring in the city's railroad sheds; another lived in Reggio di Calabria and seemed content to be operating the ferry across the strait of Messina. Their fourth son had settled in Palermo working successfully as a tourist guide while his three older brothers were searching for their fortunes and raising their families in the exciting cities of Rome, Naples and Milan. Their parents had little to worry about except for the youngest, Lucia.

Teresa sank deeper into the bed drinking in the peaceful quiet only disturbed by the flapping of the bedroom curtain. She couldn't remember when she had been so relaxed. Her heart soared! How magnificent to be free from the limits and confines of the life she had endured for so many years. Working, giving birth, working, giving birth—now her life was her own and it would be good, she was sure of it.

No need to fret about Lucia. She'd return home soon, would settle down and marry a "good Sicilian boy" as all "good Sicilian girls" had done for generations no matter what Antonio believed. Teresa and her husband were mired in their own beliefs and through the years the problem grew and festered between them. There were numerous scenes, always the same, always unpleasant and always fraught with anger. Teresa would never open her eyes to see the truth about Lucia, Antonio was convinced of it.

"Lucia's a wild girl, and it's all your fault. You always favored her over the boys."

Teresa usually countered with "she's not wild, she's just restless. You never understood her. Maybe it's because you've always favored the boys over her."

Of course it didn't matter what she said, she knew Antonio wasn't listening. The couple would glare at each other for a few tense moments and only after Antonio slammed the door following his last remark, "she'll bring disgrace on the family, you wait and see" would quiet finally flow through the house again. Teresa hated the turmoil and tried not to dwell on it. She was right about Lucia, she was sure of it.

Before Teresa made her way to her favorite bench near the garden wall she found her easel and precious box of art supplies that she had safely tucked away so long ago in a far corner of a closet seldom used. She reveled in the peace and quiet impinged on only by the air swishing through the trees. A few stray birds lingered near the statue of St. Francis. As she opened her sketchbook and began to draw, everything seemed right with the world—there was no need to worry—everything would work out.

She spent hours working on a sketch of birds feeding near St. Francis' feet and the more she worked the happier she became. As the drawing came together she felt a sense of regeneration, a feeling that she hadn't felt in a long time. She could've stayed there and worked non-stop until nightfall in the awe-inspiring silence. Perhaps that was why she hadn't heard the front door slam and Antonio shouting, "Where's my supper?" She spent the rest of the day rushing to prepare dinner and catching up on her housework all the while listening to Antonio's caustic remarks.

"I see you're back to that damn art nonsense again."

She'd learned to ignore him of course but still his remarks made her cringe. She had no way of knowing that the day that had set out to be so special was about to drift into a deep sea of disappointment.

Antonio always had had an engaging off-hand way of downplaying the significance of what he was about to say. Still Teresa wasn't prepared for the bombshell.

"I called Palermo today . . . spoke to Michael . . . told him you didn't have anything to do and he is sending his five boys for you to take care of for the rest

of the summer . . . he and Gina need a break . . . I told him to take a vacation to
the very spots he sends tourists to . . . the kids will be here tomorrow."

To say that the remainder of the summer was hell would put it mildly. The
grandsons were rambunctious. Several times one of the younger boys got into
Teresa's art supplies and smeared charcoal on several pages of her sketchbook. What pages weren't ruined were torn or creased. Many of her pastels
and charcoal pieces were broken and strewn about the garden. Once again her
art supplies were carefully stowed away in the far closet to languish there until her life was hers again. The older ones playing tag tramped through the
vegetable patch destroying most of the about-to-be-picked tomatoes. A very
precious cherub statue had been knocked over and a chubby little foot had
broken off from the cherub's leg. The statue of St. Francis was lying on its
side and the songbirds that had lingered every morning to chirp and feed at
his feet avoided the garden completely. One window was shattered by a high-
flying baseball. The house was a wreck, the garden was a wreck and Teresa
was a wreck. She'd hurt her back again lifting the youngest grandchild into
his crib and pain was now her constant companion. She knew she'd receive
no sympathy from Antonio but she tried talking to him anyway. The talks always ended bluntly.

"Ah, it's all your fault getting upset. C'mon Moma, you know boys will be
boys."

Teresa's days were filled with washing mounds of clothes lugging them outside to dry in the hot, sandy wind and cooking for her always-hungry family of
seven or more depending on who Antonio invited and he seemed to be inviting
a lot these days. Teresa felt herself sinking into an abyss of frustration and guilt
when her husband accused her of not enjoying her grandchildren.

"What kind of a grandmother complains about her grandkids?"

By the time the children left for Palermo she was exhausted. Her back was
getting worse, many of her joints were swelling and stiff and the most the
doctors advised for her arthritis was warm bath soaks.

When the calendar edged into somewhat cooler weather, Teresa was feeling worse, not the least of which was the result of Antonio's remarks that she
was "stooping just like an old lady." On an especially dreary morning she was
on the wrong side of his wicked tongue before he left for work. She couldn't
believe her ears. Antonio had called the olive plant and signed her up to return to work.

"You're good at that type of work and they need people."

He headed for the door before stopping and in his matter-of-fact way
added, "The van will pick you up in an hour."

Many life events happen by destiny, others happen by accident and for
Teresa who felt totally defeated an accident would save her day. Actually the

accident would change her life. But for now she just sat and wrestled with her thoughts. Should she be ready for the van when it came by as Antonio had ordered? Should she spend the day doing what she wanted to, working at her easel? But then, driven by fear she fretted, what would happen when Antonio returned and realized that she had defied him? Arguing with herself back and forth, the ring of the telephone jarred her back to reality. The olive plant's van had blown a tire and overturned on one of the area's winding roads. It wouldn't be able to pick her up until the following day.

Teresa felt as if she was on the brink of doing something seriously foolhardy but she went ahead with it anyway. She was not going back to work that day or any other day she explained to the voice on the phone. She tried to ignore the note of sarcasm when he replied.

"Well, I'm sure Antonio will have something to say about that. See ya' tomorrow morning."

Picking up her art supplies Teresa headed for the garden and became engrossed in her sketching. Perhaps that was why she didn't hear the sound of a car stopping in front of the house. Startled, she turned toward the soft voice calling out "Moma" and stared at Lucia.

"Papa isn't here, is he?"

Lucia stood on one foot, then the other and relief washed over her face when she was assured that her father wouldn't be home until evening. Oh, what a joy the afternoon was. Mother and daughter hugged, chatted and reveled in each other's company. They exchanged confidences while Teresa sketched and Lucia watched closely as she had done when she was a toddler. They shared memories, some pleasant, some not so pleasant. Lucia was bubbling over when she told her mother of her life in Venice. She described the busy canals, the cathedrals, the artists dotting the Piazza San Marco and the ancient elegant palaces. Lucia wanted her mother to go back with her and be at her wedding. Lucia had stars in her eyes when she spoke of Tomas. He was handsome, loving, pleasant and rich, everything she had ever wanted in a husband. Teresa tried to listen intently but her thoughts kept flying off to Antonio. She shuddered when she thought of what he would say to this news.

At least it wasn't a surprise. All evening and well into the morning hours the house was in turmoil. It was one bombshell after another. Antonio vowed to kill "the bastard." He hadn't met him, but he knew he was "no good." Lucia wouldn't go back to Venice, he'd see to that. She'd stay at home and after a reasonable amount of time Antonio would find her a good village man for a husband and that would be the end of it. The screaming, the taunts and the insults were hurled back and forth. No one gave an inch. Teresa watched the defiance in Lucia's eyes match the fire in Antonio's eyes and her thoughts spiraled back to when her daughter was a baby. She remembered how she had held her so close and sang to her every night no matter how late or tired she was. Now Lucia, her one and only daughter was about to embark on the most important event in her life and she wasn't doing it in Naso's Church of the Salvatore with all her family and friends present.

Confident that he had given Lucia the last word on the situation Antonio turned his attention to Teresa. She was to put the "damn artwork away" and go to work in the morning and take Lucia with her. When they came home, Lucia wasn't to go out of the house until he said so. He ended his tirade with "the two of you had better be home every evening when I get here." All three of them caught up in their own plans finally called it a night and fell into their beds exhausted.

No one was eager to get up a few hours later. Teresa thought everything had been said and repeated and said again but she was wrong. Lucia and her father seemed to pick up right where they had left off the night before. The more they argued the more Teresa saw what she had to do. Her daughter was not going to get married without her being there. It wasn't until Antonio left for work and peace once again reigned that the two women prepared to leave. Teresa left a note for Antonio and they closed the door behind them. In spite of her determination, Teresa still felt a sense of sadness leaving her husband and the house she had lived in for all of her married life. But she rationalized, her daughter needed her, it was the only decision she could make. And she told herself she'd be back and the whole situation would blow over. She couldn't have known what fate had in store for her.

The trip to Venice was a special delight for Teresa. The farthest she had ever been from Naso was for work at the olive plant. As they headed to Messina from a distance she watched the mist rising from Mt. Etna and marveled at its beauty. It almost seemed that the sun was painting hues of pink and purple on its summit. On and on they sped past small villages with houses made from dark-colored lava blocks a contrast to other villages with cheerful white stucco houses topped with red tiles. What a wonderful world it was and Teresa was aching to sketch all of it. Lucia turned south just before they reached Messina and they headed for the ragged coastline where a luxurious yacht was waiting.

Teresa liked Tomas from the beginning. His quick smile, his trim torso, his broad perfectly aligned shoulders and his almost shoulder-length black locks were a real eye-catcher. It was easy to see the love and devotion he and Lucia shared. This was the man her daughter was giving her heart to and Teresa felt proud. The problem back in Naso could wait for now, she was going to enjoy every minute of her visit. The next morning they pulled into a dock on the Adriatic near Venice not far from Tomas' family home.

The next few days were hectic. Lists were drawn up and items checked off. There was a special wedding dress to find, bridesmaids' finery and flowers to order. Teresa was relieved when the father of the groom mentioned that all bills should be directed to him. Lucia even had time to take her mother to a doctor and with new medicine Teresa felt better than she had in years. She had lost some of the stiffness in her joints and she was finally free of pain. She even mustered up enough courage to call Antonio and when he answered the phone he was livid. No amount of explaining her reasons for leaving helped the situation. He was not coming to his daughter's wedding and if Teresa knew what was good for her she'd get back to her husband right away.

The weeks passed quickly and one beautiful morning Teresa in an elegant new blue silk dress beamed as Tomas, looking handsome in his tuxedo and Lucia dazzling in yards and yards of satin and lace exchanged vows. The wedding was a gorgeous magical affair with all the groom's relatives and friends and Lucia's brothers and their families present. When Michael and Gina arrived Teresa, remembering her stressful summer, couldn't help but wonder where they had left their children. Antonio was conspicuous by his absence. While that was troublesome to Teresa something else was beginning to occupy her mind.

The women were different here. They were independent and voiced their opinions whether they agreed with their husbands or not. While they worked together raising their children the women wouldn't have accepted harsh orders from their husbands. It was all so far removed from the life Teresa had endured for so many years. One lazy afternoon while she and Lucia were basking in the sun they discussed Antonio. Mother and daughter had always been close and now it seemed as if they were drawing even closer.

"You know Moma, Papa's just a mean-spirited bully. That's why I wanted to get you away from him. Listen to me, you don't have to take that kind of treatment Moma."

Teresa wondered if her daughter was right. Still, attitudes don't change overnight and even though she marveled at Lucia's wisdom at times her thoughts returned to Naso and Antonio.

For the next few months Teresa rationalized that she was remaining in Venice to take advantage of her new doctor and the thermal baths that he had ordered. Antonio was not convinced she needed any medical attention. Then Teresa argued that she had to stay until Lucia no longer needed her. Well, not really. The new bride was happy and building a career at one of the local television stations. Antonio was not convinced that his daughter, "who had disgraced the family" needed anyone.

Teresa knew she'd have to return to Naso eventually but she decided she needed to stay "just a little longer" to prepare for one of the city's art festivals. She had become a permanent fixture at the Piazza San Marco. Tomas would accompany her there in the morning and take her home in the evening until she felt comfortable traveling alone on the waterbus. Thus her day was spent sketching the piazza sights from every angle. On sunny days she'd concentrate on the Basilica with its five hundred stately marble columns, the Doge's Palace with its graceful archways and gaze out to capture the gray-green peaceful waters of the Adriatic.

Rainy weather brought her inside the elegant buildings to sketch ancient mosaics, gilded ceilings and statuary that took her breath away. She soon became a part of the circle of artists who frequented the piazza toting their palettes and easels always helping, suggesting and encouraging each other. When she received the second prize at the art festival they were there for her and cheered the loudest.

Teresa was happier than she had been in years but she was running out of excuses to remain in Venice. More than once Antonio had slammed the phone down when she called. One late afternoon a group of tourists strolling through the piazza clustered around her, their interest piqued by her capture of the setting sun's light reflecting off the Basilica's four lunettes. People behind her had never bothered her before but now she felt a sense of uneasiness. The tourists drifted off but Teresa still felt the presence of one. When she casually turned she came face to face with Antonio.

He looked dirty and disheveled. They moved to an outdoor café and talked, about everything and yet nothing. More than once he mentioned that the house was a mess, the laundry hadn't been done and he hadn't had "a decent meal" since she left. The villagers were asking about her, they couldn't believe she'd "left her husband and run off to Venice." She and her daughter had "disgraced the family" and the parish priest and the nuns were praying for her every day to return to her senses, "to come back and be a good wife." He was convinced that her "damn artwork" and caused all their troubles.

"But I am a forgiving person, you can come home and that will be the end of it." Then he cautioned her, "You know you can't get along without me."

She gave him her full attention and she saw a stranger, she'd lived with, loved with, argued with for decades and yet she'd never really known him. When she finally had a chance to speak her voice had an unfamiliar tone in it.

"Antonia I've changed, I'm happy in Venice. I guess I'm saying I'm not coming back now."

They stared at each other for a long moment and she watched his stunned reaction. To a casual passerby they were just two people sitting at a café table catching glimpses of each other in the muted light of a candle's flame in the Piazza San Marco trying to reach each other and failing badly. Teresa began to empty the thoughts that had been festering inside her for so long. She described how Tomas' relatives and friends were living, equal partners in marriages of love and devotion not one partner submissive and the other domineering and cruel. He appeared to listen but suddenly his attention shifted to the couple making their way towards them.

Worried about Teresa, Lucia and Tomas had come to the piazza to find her. Teresa was sure her heart had stopped, Antonio had fire in his eyes. His glare darted from Tomas, to Lucia to Teresa and back again in dead silence. Finally Antonio spoke. He was taking his wife back "to where she should be." Tomas and Lucia turned to Teresa. Her son-in-law was hoping she'd stay in Venice for Lucia's sake. Lucia was hoping her mother would stay in Venice and build a new life for her own sake. Teresa at that point still felt she might return to Naso in the far distant future. Antonio left shortly afterwards and with his last grave remark ringing in her ears it became apparent that their marriage would no longer be the same.

"If you stay here any longer I won't forgive you and you won't have any place to come home to."

Teresa had much to occupy her mind the next few months. Cold chills traveled down her back when she thought of returning to her old life, the same life that her mother and grandmother and all her female ancestors had lived. She wished she could talk to them and tell them that with the help of her daughter she had reached deep inside herself to find independence and a sense of self worth.

Time moved on. Teresa and Antonio spoke occasionally but there were more than geographical miles keeping them apart. Antonio in a particularly poignant moment told her that he "didn't know any other way to act" and she wondered if she could ever change back to the woman he needed and wanted. And while the human heart has a tremendous capacity to love and to forgive, the blind love that Teresa had for Antonio was fading.

Is there really one decisive moment when one abruptly changes or is it the result of a tiny pinpoint of light that begins every so slowly in one's mind before it erupts into complete acceptance that change has occurred—the past is gone and there is no turning back? Teresa's transformation did not come easy or quickly but it did come when she faced the fact that away from Antonio she no longer felt suffocated. Yet in her own way at times she'd recall the memories of the times they had had together but even those thoughts lessened with time.

It seems as if all the tensions of the past years have melted into a deepening joy. Teresa's artwork is shown on television and is framed in the homes of influential Venetians and she's become a full-fledged member of Tomas' family. Lucia had opened the door for her to a grand new life where she is her own person not just a second-class being fulfilling the overpowering social expectations of her husband and her village. Teresa and Lucia hope that their example will help other women overcome their preconceived notions that the life of their grandmothers and mothers is not the way their life has to be, rather that marriage should be partnership not a command and control relationship. And their wish is that others of their gender will find fulfillment in their own unique talents.

Chapter Eight

"Where I was born and where and how I have lived is unimportant. It is what I have done and where I have been that should be of interest."

—Georgia O'Keefe

Larisa had stayed up most of the night anxiously pacing back and forth. As far back as she could remember she had always been thrilled with the area's "White Nights," but now the over twenty hours of sunlight each day meant little more to her than giving the glowing night sky a passing glance.

Growing up in Petrozavodsk had meant gathering with her friends to see how many days and illuminated nights during the first days of summer they could stay awake. The young people would laugh and gossip and flirt as they made the rounds of the numerous nonstop parties and dances until the revelry ended when they could no longer forgo sleep. And the tradition had continued with her daughters, Marsha and Tatayana. Now both young women were coming home for a visit for their mother's fiftieth birthday and while Larisa was excited at having her little family together again she was also apprehensive about how they would accept the news she was about to spring on them.

Marsha, her oldest girl, petite and graceful with beautiful soft blonde-white hair had trained for years at the Karelian Republic's acclaimed Conservatory of Music and when she left Petrozavodsk for the White Night Festival in St. Petersburg she was well equipped to perform as a top ballet dancer. That was nearly five years ago and Marsha had remained in Russian's beautiful "cultural capital" and soon became a favorite performer at the city's several concert halls. She had a satisfying career and had married well. Her wealthy and handsome husband Rodion was a well-known local government official and a devoted patron of the arts in St. Petersburg. Marsha's sporadic notes and phone calls to her mother gave no indication that her daughter's life was anything but happy and fulfilling.

At the terminal Marsha jostled through the crowd and reached her train a few short minutes before it inched out of the station to begin its daily nine-hour run to Petrozavodsk. One could not help but notice her as she settled into her compartment. Her fine black Italian leather luggage and soft, elegant gray chinchilla coat spoke of living well and her confident air was hard to ignore. Still many times in life nothing is as it appears to be. A fellow traveler could not have known that Marsha was dangling between two worlds, the world of St. Petersburg with its inspiring cultural events and thrilling night life and the world beyond that she longed to be a part of.

The sun danced across the scratches on the compartment's windows as the train chugged eastward. Marsha appeared to be studying the high wispy clouds as they folded and unfolded overhead signaling a storm in the distance. However she was not thinking of the sky, her thoughts were elsewhere. She had traveled back to her wedding day when she and Rodion, along with family and friends met at The House, that very special red brick building on the edge of Lake Onega. The structure had been the scene of many romantic weddings for as long as anyone could remember and while hopes were high for lasting marriages there were those who for whatever reasons, had dissolved their unions. Tradition called for them to formally end their marriages by throwing their wedding rings into the lake. Marsh sighed and closed her eyes in an attempt to doze. She was in high spirits to see her mother and sister again, yet she was apprehensive at the news she was about to spring on them.

Tatayana was still in a deep sleep or one might say a deep stupor. They had had another long night of parties and had consumed more than their share of vodka along with the usual hard drugs. The young woman hated how she felt in the mornings, actually she hated how she felt most of the day but Oleg insisted that they "live life to the fullest." Oleg, her lover for the past two years had introduced her to the "good life" in Moscow. He never spoke of his livelihood and Tatayana didn't pry but she had a good idea the source of his income. She enjoyed his lavish apartment, the flashy imported cars, the chic clothes and the impressive dacha a few hours drive into the countryside, the scene of many clandestine meetings.

She became adept at ignoring the late night strange gatherings when Oleg and his business partners shut themselves up in his study behind an unusually odd looking steel door to discuss their business ventures which usually ended with the distribution of modified weapons. And if by chance a Moscow businessman or two were found dead in some out of the way spot a few days later it didn't mean that it was Oleg's doing and anyway, Tatayana reasoned, she wasn't involved, so it was none of her business.

Moscow hadn't been kind to her when she first arrived in the city. Although trained as a fashion designer she was still unemployed and practically broke six months after she'd left Petrozavodsk. As Russia's new rich became more fashion conscious, the industry was beginning to burst open. However, to

Tatayana's dismay, jobs were usually given to a select few, those with connections to certain crime families.

Tatayana, completely discouraged was about to discard her dreams of working and living in Moscow. She was just a week or two away from eviction from her sparse room when Oleg spotted her with her case of sketches on a street corner waiting for a trolley car and he liked what he saw. She was a real beauty. Tall and svelte, her long chestnut hair gleamed in the afternoon sun. A master at makeup she knew how to draw attention to her striking dark eyes and full ruby-red lips. Always fond of clothes she had the ability to make a plain ordinary dress look elegant with just the right accessories. With Oleg's promise that he'd take care of her and "when the time's right" he'd use his connections to find her a position in the fashion world, she moved into his apartment and the young couple became part of each other's lives — at least that is what Tatayana thought. Whenever she reminded him of his promise he'd soothe over the discussion with "it'll take a little longer, just act like you're on vacation."

At first she was flattered by Oleg's behavior. She felt he loved her and since she was madly in love with him she followed his instructions when he told her what to wear, how to act, what to say and when to say it. By the time she realized that she'd lost all control over her life she had slipped headlong down that long dark tunnel of drug addiction and her life was slowly becoming a living hell. Their daily arguments plummeted into daily violence and more than once a doctor was summoned to the apartment to mend a broken wrist, treat a busted lip or stitch a slashed arm or shoulder.

Tatayana wasn't sure what had finally got to her. Perhaps it was the pleasant days and nights gone bad, very bad. Perhaps it was the physical and emotional abuse. Maybe it was Oleg's command that she have an abortion without considering her feelings. Perhaps it was his eagerness to supply her with drugs that it all collapsed in on her. She felt trapped in a war zone and more than once pondered if suicide was the only way out. Of course, Tatayana had no way of knowing that fate was soon to give her a hand.

Several nights later after an eerie call well after midnight that Tatayana was too drugged to understand, Oleg hurriedly flung a few clothes into a suitcase and departed for Istanbul. As the next evening approached the fog in Tatayana's head slowly cleared. Suddenly she sat up in bed as Oleg's last words rolled around her head.

"I don't know when I'll be back but you'd better be here waiting for me. You don't even need to leave the apartment; I've got you stocked up on everything."

In a flash she realized what she had to do. Her mind was churning faster and faster. She could leave now! Yes, that was it. She'd leave and never come back! She was tired of the drinking bouts, the drugs and the violence — all she could think of was Petrozavodsk and home. Before long she had boarded a trolley car, its destination the Moscow train terminal. As with most of the transportation system in Russia's capital, the trolley car was a relic of harsher times. While still working it groaned and screeched and rocked back and forth and when it lurched to a stop the unoccupied seats tilted forward.

Perhaps it was the swaying movement of the crumbling and dilapidated trolley as it crisscrossed the streets of Moscow. Perhaps it was the excesses of vodka combined with the drugs but soon Tatayana was ill, sicker than she'd ever been. It seemed as if her head and her stomach were each pulling in different directions. Finally the terminal's outline lay a few short blocks ahead. Inside to her dismay, she found that the last train of the day had already left.

Tatayana knew that returning to the apartment was not an option but she had no choice. She bought her ticket for the first eleven hour run the following morning and settled in to spend the night in the terminal.

It would be a night Tatayana would never forget. She found a somewhat comfortable out-of-the way chair and endured the terrible chills, those moments when she felt so cold she was unable to stop shivering. Other times it was as if hundreds of hot burning flames were racing through her body and beads of perspiration broke out across her forehead. She never strayed far from the restroom and although she hadn't eaten she was still retching.

As dawn's first light filtered through the tall gray terminal windows, Tatayana somewhat unsteadily reached her train. She dissolved into her seat and dozed more for the need to escape than the need to sleep. Frightening thoughts were banging around in her head as the train pulled out of the station. She worried about Oleg finding her and she worried about how her mother and sister would greet the news she was about to spring on them.

Larisa and Marsha hurried along the terminal's platform scanning each window for signs of Tatayana as her train gradually edged into the station. Indeed she would have missed her stop had not a train employee noticed her slouched down in her seat and shook her awake. She had hoped to have enough time to apply make-up to her facial scars but it was too late. Still in the excitement of the moment she figured that her mother and sister mightn't notice.

What a homecoming it was! A passerby could not have felt the anxiety underneath the general pleasure of a mother and her two daughters finally together again hugging, laughing and crying and all speaking at once. Enjoying the bright light of night they talked and gossiped and relived old memories for hours. They were drifting into an overall sense of bonding and warmth, this was more than a birthday reunion, it would become a time of transformation and support as the three women confided in each other the pain and the joy of their lives.

Tatayana prayed they wouldn't notice her wobbly gait as they climbed the deep steps to enter the apartment that had been home to all three of them for so many years. They gathered around the small red Formica kitchen table that had seen its share of happy meals and some non-so happy family gatherings. As the hours ticked by Larisa was more and more hesitant to barrel right into her news but her daughters made the step easier by asking, "Where's Papa?" They had to strain to hear her answer.

"Your father and I are . . . well . . . we're . . . no longer married," she finally blurted out. "We divorced several months ago."

She searched her daughters' faces to catch their reaction to her news. She saw startled eyes and heard gasps and then braced herself for their probing questions. How could they not be married? They were the foundation of their family and now that foundation had been torn asunder. Sure they knew that their father was absent most of the time but they attributed that to his career choice. He was a military man and had lived at various bases through the years, still when he was home they were a real family, weren't they?

Larisa continued nonstop and touched on a subject she wished she didn't have to. She had to root around in her heart for the right words to tell them.

"Your father, well . . . he . . . he . . . was an . . . adulterer . . . and well . . . that issue stayed with us through the years . . . in spite of all your father's promises . . . promises I know now that he never intended to keep. Sure I put up with it when you girls were growing up . . . but after you both left . . . well . . . one day I just came to the realization that what appeared to the outside world as a loving marriage was just a terrible farce."

Larisa was crying softly now, "I just couldn't accept his affairs any longer. I just couldn't."

She told about the pain she'd endured for so long and how it was that very pain that caused her to evaluate her life. She spoke of how she reached deep inside herself to muster the courage to enter nursing school but then when she did she fell into an abyss of self-doubts with those gnawing 'what ifs' that always seemed to be swirling around in her head. She dried her tears and forced a smile as she continued.

"What if I couldn't make it on my own? What if I was just taking on more than I could handle? And then I'd argue with myself—in spite of all the affairs was it right to throw away a marriage that had endured for almost thirty years?"

Heavy tension lay across the small room before she took a deep breath and joked about her first day of training.

"Here I was, older than any of my fellow classmates, but that's not all, I soon realized that I was old enough to be a mother to most of my professors."

She finished her studies, became a full-fledged pediatric nurse and "that was that." Then as if to rationalize her decision in the eyes of her daughters one last time she decided to add her last remark.

"Oh, girls, your father had this deeper darker side of him that I always shielded you from."

No one stirred as if to allow it all to sink in. Finally Marsha and Tatayana stood up and reached for their mother.

"You should've told us Ma," Tatayana said and Marsha's head nodded in agreement. "We could've helped you."

Larisa held them close and added, "it's a long time since I've been as happy."

Her last statement seemed to signal that for now the subject was closed and everyone breathed a sigh of relief, that is everyone except Tatayana.

"Oh, Ma" she whispered, "I wish I could say I was happy . . . You've probably . . . well, you've probably noticed the marks on my face and neck."

Well, yes she had and so had her sister but as tempted as they were to push for an immediate explanation each of them had decided to wait until Tatayana was ready to talk.

She began speaking slowly in a muffled voice almost as if she didn't speak loud enough perhaps it hadn't happened. But it had of course and even though she was buried under layers of shame and guilt she didn't hold anything back. Larisa and Marsha found it hard to believe what they were hearing as the whole sordid truth was exposed, the drunken parties, the drugs, the shady dealings of her lover, their lives running amok and finally her escape from it all.

"I can never go back. I don't know what's to become of me. Oh, I'm so . . . so ashamed."

She was totally defeated and gave such a deep sigh that her shoulders sagged.

"Well, I know what's to become of you. I'm going to take you to the hospital to be examined and treated. I know most of the doctors there and I know they can help you." Larisa had shifted into her motherly role. "Then when you feel better you'll find a job and get your career going. Your courage and your determination will see you through this."

When she saw the defeat linger in Tatayana's eyes she added, "We're here for you, you know that. Things will be better you'll see." Just when Larisa was sounding so optimistic Tatayana stood up and stumbled into the bathroom. When Larisa heard her ill daughter's retching and crying it became painfully realistic that getting Tatayana well again would be no short-term project. Mother and sister hovered over the sick young woman, helping her into bed and piling on the blankets until she stopped shivering. Larisa pulled down the dark shades and motioned to Marsha.

"Perhaps we should get an hour or two of sleep. We've had quite an overwhelming day."

The troubled mother had no idea she was about to be blindsided by another crisis.

"Not yet Ma. I have something that's eating at me that I need to share. Rodion and I had a horrible fight before I left. I really don't know what's going to happen now. . . everything's so mixed up."

Marsha's career was going well in Petersburg, after many performances she was happy to announce that she'd become the toast of the town. Rodion was proud of her, she knew that. Indeed he never tired of seeing her dance and most performances he was in his favorite first balcony box seat. Then out of the blue an opportunity presented itself. She had only to say the word and she'd be touring with a ballet company that was going to perform in the most prestigious opera and concerts halls in Paris, Brussels, Vienna, Rome and Florence. To Marsha's chagrin Rodion was against it—totally against it. They argued and fought and some days never spoke or even acknowledged each other.

"Ma, I haven't been any further than Petersburg. I want to see the world, dance for the world. I'm going, I've got to. I told him I didn't care if he liked it or not."

Marsha began to pace back and forth as she continued.

"I know we said some terrible things to each other, I even accused him of keeping me in a cage like a bird. When I left to come here I didn't even leave him a note telling him when I'd be back."

Her voice trailed off.

"I love him, oh, I do, but now. . . am I wrong, have I really made a mess of things?" With a long sigh she added, "maybe he's right. I should just be happy with what I've got."

"No, you haven't Marsha. It'll work out you'll see. Rodion is a good man—he's a fair man. He'll see what's best for both of you and beside that he loves you, you know that."

Marsh didn't share Larisa's convictions but she was too exhausted to do anything but fall into bed. For hours the three women had shared their lives and their hurts and sobbed over them. They weren't sure what lay ahead but they knew they were there for each other no matter what happened.

Several hours later Larisa was in the kitchen dabbing tears from her eyes while busily preparing rice soup for Tatayana. Her precious daughter looked so vulnerable in the bed, her body marked and full of bruises and her face swollen from excess alcohol use. When she moved Tatayana's luggage, pills spilled across the floor, blue and white pills, red and white ones, others the color of saffron along with a small plastic bag filled with white powder all giving evidence of addiction. At first she planned to flush them away but stopped abruptly when she realized that it was her daughter who would have to do that.

Today was hardly a day that Larisa had bargained for to celebrate her fiftieth birthday but she put on her public face and went through the motions. She donned her best dress, greeted her relatives and friends in the apartment building's meeting room and served them cake and vodka. Even though she appeared to join their laughter as they traded stories of the many experiences they had had through the years, her thoughts were on her sick daughter upstairs. When the last guest left Marsha and Larisa looked in on Tatayana hoping that she would be well enough to join them when they strolled to The

House on the lake. When she appeared to be in a deep restful sleep they departed without her.

The delightful fragrance of freshly cut flowers meshed with the aroma of soft flickering votive candles and gave the inside of the red brick building a romantic air. Beaming couples dressed in their best finery exchanged wedding rings before family and friends. But there were one or two others there also, stern faced individuals standing aside and buried in their own thoughts while following the age-old tradition of throwing their rings into the lake as a symbolic gesture of ended marriages. Larisa closed her eyes for a moment before she followed suit and then Lake Onega had another ring sinking to its bottom joining the cache of rings that had been added through the years. When she turned to leave she looked radiant. She'd never been as proud of herself as she was at that moment. Now she felt as if she was truly her own woman.

Mother and daughter strolled past the ferry dock and lingered for a few brief moments to watch the hydrofoils packed with high-spirited locals and tourists arriving to celebrate the White Nights. They were almost home when Larisa and Marsha agreed that if Tatayana hadn't improved they'd take her to the hospital.

Larisa made her way up the long staircase while Marsha stopped in the meeting room to gather the flowers and table decorations, remnants of the afternoon's birthday festivities. With the lights turned off and the draperies drawn the room had taken on a dark and dismal air. While she searched for the light switch a door at the far end of the room slowly the door inched open and a tall man entered and moved towards her.

"I guess I missed the party."

Marsha glanced over her shoulder and her face went white. Rodion, his arms full of two lavish bouquets of pink and white roses stood before her. They stared at each other for what seemed an eternity before Rodion finally spoke somewhat sheepishly.

"One of these is for your mother. Did she have a happy birthday?" When she found her breath Marsha spoke of Tatayana and all the events that had happened since she'd left Petersburg. Rodion and Marsha knew they'd have to talk about the rift between them but they didn't want to go there yet. The next hour was spent at the hospital anxiously waiting for the doctors' verdict about Tatayana that proved more upsetting than earlier feared. They listened and had to deal with "liver damage due to drugs and excess alcohol." Yes, her physical bruises would heal, "but the emotional bruises will take much longer." Larisa remained at the hospital. Actually it would be the first of her many nights there. Marsha and Rodion promising to return in the morning left and found an isolated bench at the water's edge to talk and attempt to mend their marriage.

Rodion began first, he loved her—loved her dearly—sure he understood that she'd worked hard for her career—but her place was in their Petersburg home together. Plain and simple he didn't want her to go on tour. Marsha sat in silence. Her heart was about to break. Her husband hadn't budged an inch. She had no choice as she began to talk so softly that her words were almost carried away with the light breeze moving in from the lake.

She loved him—loved him dearly—he was the love of her life—she didn't want to break up their marriage but "I have to do this Rodion." It was plain and simple, she was leaving in a few days to begin the tour. No one spoke for several minutes they were both searching their hearts and souls for an end to the impasse.

With the apartment all to themselves the young couple spent a delightfully sensual night making love and dozing in each other's arms. It would be a night both of them would long remember. While Marsha was dressing, Rodion came up behind her and held her close.

"I know this tour is important for you so . . . I guess . . . Well, I guess I'll be making a lot of trips on the weekends."

What could have happened? Could it have been Marsha's question to her husband earlier, a question many women must ask of their husbands.

"If you had to travel in your job would I have the right to say no, you can't go?"

Could it have been the open page of a popular tourist publication that caught Rodion's eye as it listed the regular flights and new ones being initiated almost weekly from St. Petersburg to many of the larger European cities?

Even after more than a decade of being able to travel abroad freely, Rodion couldn't forget that for most of his life, foreign travel was viewed with suspicion or in some cases was outright denied when the country was under the Communist thumb. It was no secret that some of the brave souls who had dared to apply for a visa in the past received harsh treatment and lengthy interrogations. Now Russians were freer than they'd ever been and to be able to go and come as one wished was still taking some getting used to.

As the weeks have moved on Marsha and the troupe are the toast of Europe. Rodion travels to Paris, Brussels, and Vienna and a trip to Florence and Rome remains on the horizon. He is never prouder of his wife than when she is the recipient of dozens and dozens of gorgeous roses and other flower arrangements that grace her dressing room, tokens of adoration from appreciative audiences.

Larisa's career is progressing and has made her feel a complete woman. One only has to glance at her to sense her inner happiness. She continues to be a source of inspiration to her coworkers, many in the same predicament as she was in with a marriage, in name only, that was robbing her of her self-esteem.

Tatayana continues to move ahead in her fight against addiction. She has a teaching position waiting for her as a instructor of fashion design at the local technical institute even as she lives in fear that Oleg might find her someday and force her back to their old lifestyle. She needn't worry. Rumor has it that his body was found in an isolated warehouse in a seedy part of Istanbul, no doubt the result of a drug deal gone badly.

The threads of these three women's lives continue to mesh tightly together. While proud of their own achievements they also savor each other's triumphs. They are comforted by the fact that when life's journey gets a bit ragged, they are there for each other. They are part of the global sisterhood for when one woman overcomes adversity her example can flutter across the world and give inspiration to us all.

Chapter Nine

"To be nobody but yourself—in a world which is doing its best, night and day, to make you everybody else—means to fight the hardest battle which any human being can fight, and never stop fighting."

—e.e. commings.

Olivia awoke to the slam of a door on the upper floor of her small dormitory nestled behind a row of massive oak trees. More students leaving for summer break she mumbled to herself as she bounded out of bed. She peered out the window as she had done every morning for the past three years. She'd been happy and content here near the university and away from the clatter and distractions of downtown Barcelona, one of Spain's grandest cities. She'd used her time well to immerse herself in her studies and earn accolades and letters of recommendations from many of her professors. A slight smile crossed her face as she thought of her friends and how they had teased her that she'd surely worn a path from her room to the lecture halls to the university library and back again. Well, that was O.K. she reasoned—her friends didn't have to justify being where they were nor did they have their lives planned out for them down to the smallest detail.

She dressed quickly, threw a few things in a suitcase and hastily made her way to the city's busiest terminal, still largely empty due to the early hour. She was the first passenger on the bus and impatient to get going. After today, if everything went well, she'd be able to move on with her life. The bus, laboring under the weight of assorted bags, suitcases and beach gear and filled to capacity with happy travelers, finally edged out onto the highway. Olivia's eyes ran over the passengers. Some of them were in a jovial mood looking forward to a few fun-filled days at the beach and the opportunity to sample plenty of San Sebastian's nightlife. Others with sleepy toddlers in tow were planning on attending the city's festival on Sunday.

Childhood memories floated through her mind and she remembered how excited she'd been on festival days. The gala meant jostling through the decorated and crowded streets with her father and sister to find the perfect spot to eye the processions and the oversized figures in brilliant reds and dazzling bright yellow costumes hobbling awkwardly along. She thought back to how she'd been frightened by some of the participants wearing giant papier-mache heads. And she also remembered standing quiet and reverent as some of the local men moved solemnly beneath holy banners with bold strokes of color while others carried a platform with a full scale statue of the Virgin on their shoulders. She laughed to herself at the custom she and her friends had followed during the festivals. The young girls would pick out a man from the parade that they hoped to marry someday. Oh, how they'd giggle and whisper as they compared their choices. That was where she first caught sight of Marco, so tall, so dark and, so handsome.

Olivia turned to catch a last glimpse of Barcelona's beautiful skyline dotted with the many churches' steeples and especially the towering façade of the cathedral. As she watched it all fade slowly in the distance she vowed to be back. She couldn't have known that the vow she'd made would play havoc with the two relationships she valued the most.

It seemed as if everything reminded her of Marco today. As the bus headed west and skirted the Pyrenees she thought of the many breathtaking hikes she and Marco had had on the vibrant light to dark green foothills searching for the perfect spot to be alone with their picnic basket crammed with Sangria and goat cheese. Before she left for Barcelona they had been inseparable, when not hiking they spent exciting days at the beach swimming, riding the waves and sunny themselves. Olivia knew that she was the envy of her friends. One look at Marco and one could see immediately that he was dedicated to fitness. He spent many hours on weightlifting and jogging and had many ribbons to prove it. He looked terrific in his swimming trunks. Actually he looked terrific in anything. He was always ready to party, especially if he could be the life of the party.

The only argument that she could remember was the ongoing one they had a few days before she left San Sebastian. Marco couldn't understand why they couldn't get married right then and there, couldn't understand why her father had vehemently said no marriage until his youngest daughter (and his favorite) reached her twenty-first birthday. Not surprising, her father was more interested to see what Marco would make of himself. More than once he had sarcastically wondered aloud how far Marco could get being a beach bum working a few weeks here and there before returning to the sand and sun and the Bay of Biscay's soft waves. But there was more, Marco just couldn't understand Olivia's passion for books and learning. She was going to be his "wife for god's sake, and that should be enough."

It was the same every day from morning to late at night Olivia pleading and Marco threatening.

"What makes you think I'll wait for you to get over this book thing?"

And more than once Olivia would give him a straight answer.

"If you love me you'll wait."

Disgusted at her reply he'd head for the water and disappear into the biggest wave he could find. Of course he wasn't the only problem Olivia had. Her father wasn't all that keen on her going to Barcelona's university but it was the best solution at the time. Whatever their conversations led they always seemed to end the same.

"Dear Olivia, my beautiful daughter, you'll be back here working at the restaurant and you'll be the prettiest hostess we ever had."

The city was full of restaurants and gourmet eateries but the Inn at San Sebastian was the one most raved about by natives and tourists alike. The beautiful structure with a Moorish design, striking frescos, marble columns and velvet-upholstered furniture had been in the family for generations. While most of the large extended family was employed in various endeavors at the Inn, Olivia's father, Eduardo Aguirre was in charge.

Olivia had worked as a hostess a few weeks each summer in between classes and she detested the job. Checking reservations, turning people away when the Inn was filled to capacity, sitting people at the available tables and secluded booths and then listening to them complain about the view.

"We can't see the ocean from here."

It wasn't easy keeping a smile frozen across her face as she searched for a different site for the complainers while hoping the new table would be more to their liking. She learned to keep her pleasant demeanor when overhearing grumbling from other patrons that their table didn't have enough candles, while others claimed their table had too many candles. Of course, there were other warm and gracious patrons who praised the gourmet food and the courteous service but Olivia had decided that this wasn't her idea of a perfect job and it certainly was not what she wanted for the rest of her life. Each year she'd double up on summer school classes to have as little time as possible away from the university and working at home in the Inn. Several times her father could be heard talking to his business partners and questioning if Olivia really "needed to take all those summer classes."

The past year Marco's letters and phone calls had become less frequent. And while Olivia was concerned about this noticeable inattention, she figured that everything would be worked out when she and Marco were together again. She'd outline her plan to her handsome lover, engage in some fast-talking and convince him that he'd just adore living in Barcelona. Her father would agree to her marriage now that she was twenty-one and Marco and she would have the most beautiful wedding. And of course, they'd find the perfect apartment and while she was at her classes Marco would find the right job and begin a successful career just what her father predicted would never happen.

While all this was flying around in Olivia's mind Marco was pondering how to bury his behavior for the past year. Rumors had darted across the city about his dalliance with a young attractive and wealthy English widow. And as if that wasn't enough there had also been gossip that he'd been living off and on in an impressive villa overlooking the ocean with one of the country's most glamorous models. Several times in the past few weeks he'd been seen sniffing cocaine at parties and gatherings and rumors had it that Marco was the one to contact for the drug.

Well, he'd just deny all of it. Everything would be fine, he reasoned. While he once had wanted marriage, it was the last thing on his mind now. He enjoyed his lifestyle, it was the life for him. Of course, he might have to go through the motions but he'd make the sacrifice and walk down the aisle to make Olivia his bride if that's what it took. He laughed to himself, as the son-in-law he'd get a job at the Inn and it would be the perfect place to make contacts for his many shady business ventures. Nothing to worry about he decided. After all, he had plenty of experience in the "sweet talk" department and he liked to think that he hadn't met a woman yet whom he couldn't charm and anyway he and Olivia always picked up where they had left off when she returned for a short visit. And so he shrugged, "what could go wrong?"

It hadn't been easy for Olivia to keep her plans a secret from everyone. More than once she was ready to tell her father that at the urging of some of her professors she had applied to law school, passed the entrance exam with flying colors, had been accepted and was looking forward to classes beginning in a few weeks. While all this was going on Olivia's father was pondering why she was so evasive as to when she'd leave Barcelona for good. But on the other hand he figured no need to press it now, everything would be worked out when she returned to home.

Olivia dozed off thinking how delighted everyone would be when she arrived but she had to admit to herself her anxiety level was rising. Would all the hugging and good cheer vanish in a flash when her father learned of her plans? She drew her brief case closer and thought about what was inside. Actually what was inside the case was her life, copies of her letters of recommendation, her transcript, a copy of her law school application and its accompanying acceptance letter. She thought back to the many nights she'd sat by her window in the dorm staring out at the old oak trees their limbs heavy with the evening dew and mulled over all the problems and all the rewards of her decision.

As the bus rolled along she tuned out its monotonous hum, the sound of lighthearted chatter and the fussiness of the children and fell asleep. When she'd awaken she'd be face to face with San Sebastian and all that that entailed.

While the bus was winging its way westward a scene was being played out in the grand resort city that would affect all their lives. Marco had received a call from an old girlfriend, Gina Valladez asking him to drop by her house. No problem, he thought, I'll just jog over there and then hop on over to the bus station to surprise Olivia. He couldn't have known that Gina's house was filling up fast with a few very important people who were ready to pounce on him. There was Gina's parents, the parish priest Father Juan, the local Police Chief Francisco Diego and one of his assistants, Miguel (not surprising he was Gina's older brother) who stood sternly at the door with his arms folded across his chest.

One look at Gina's face and anyone could tell that she had spent most of the last few days and nights crying. Her eyes were red, her face was swollen and her uncombed hair was a mess. Marco didn't endure himself to anyone when he lightheartedly announced he'd just be able to stay for a few minutes as he had another appointment. The air was thick with overwhelmingly smoldering resentments and Marco's last statement was the spark that set the room on fire. Suddenly everyone was on their feet shouting and desperately trying to have his or her particular grievance heard.

Gina was pregnant. Marco was the only one who could be the father. Gina had sinned but would be made pure again after confession. Marco would burn in hell for his misdeeds and last but certainly not least Police Chief Diego announced he had a warrant for Marco's arrest on cocaine smuggling charges.

Father Juan was pleading with everyone to keep calm but nobody seemed to be listening. The Valladez's were cursing their daughter's lover. Gina was sobbing as never before and the Police Chief ordered Miguel to put handcuffs on Marco. Miguel as you can imagine was very happy to comply before brusquely shoving the prisoner into the police wagon and speeding off to the city's jail. Father Juan recited a few prayers for the troubled family and took his leave. Only then did a peaceful quiet drift through the house occasionally interrupted by Gina's sporadic sobs. Thus the young girl and her parents were left to deal with a situation that none of them wanted.

While Marco was going through the motions of getting booked on the drug charges a few short blocks away Olivia was lightheartedly claiming her luggage and hailing a taxi. Impatient to confront her father she went directly to the Inn. It was a slow night for the restaurant and her father, seeing his favorite daughter standing at the door, shouted out.

"There she is. There she is. Olivia come over here."

In between hugs he announced, "my pretty Olivia, home to stay at last." He was beaming as he turned to the locals and the tourists.

"You'll be seeing a lot of this pretty gal she's going to be our new hostess."

As the bar crowd cheered, Olivia soon realized that it was neither the time nor the place to have a serious discussion with her father. She just played along with a slight smile moving across her face and headed for the kitchen to see her sister, Clarita, the only one who always referred to Olivia as Liv. Clarita had recently been promoted to Chief Pastry Chef and she enjoyed her position and loved every minute of her day creating wonderful pastries and gorgeous cakes for weddings, christenings, family reunions and other special occasions.

It was great to be together again, the two sisters agreed. But as Clarita was finishing her last batch of churros for the day Olivia felt an uneasiness seeping into their conversation when she jokingly inquired about the latest local gossip. Maybe it was just her imagination she reasoned when Clarita clammed up and then in a somewhat cryptic tone directed her younger sister to go home.

"Liv wait for me there. I've really got some important things, really important things to share with you."

Olivia didn't have long to ponder Clarita's orders. The young traveler became distracted as the kitchen door suddenly swung open and she was surrounded by a full complement of cousins, all engaged in various endeavors as bartenders, waiters, busboys and kitchen help, their lives all revolving around the Inn. There was plenty of hugs and good-natured ribbing.

"So, how's life in Barcelona?"

"So what does a pretty college gal like you do with your spare time?" and "glad to see you're home for good now."

The last remark made her flinch. Eventually her father rescued her from the group and they both headed for home. Thus father and daughter bound so tightly in their own dreams for the future strolled arm and arm to the comfortable old home that had been in family for over a hundred years. They couldn't have known that the turmoil of the next few hours would create bitter feelings and a string of unexpected events not easily forgotten.

Once inside father and daughter headed for the grand old dining room full of so many heartwarming memories. Olivia thought of the early years sitting on a high-backed chair stacked with thick books to reach the huge mahogany table, her feet barely touching the floor as she completed her homework under the watchful eye of her father. The room had been the scene of many joyful family gatherings, she could almost hear all the laughter and good cheer that had been bounded about during the years. But the room was also a sad place. It was here that her father had lifted her and Clarita on his lap, held them close and forcing back his tears told them of their mother's death. Maria Aguirre had gone to Madrid to visit her sister Magadelena and on the return trip had failed to make a sharp turn on a winding road on the outskirts of the capital. While years had passed the loss was still with all of them. They couldn't pass the fireplace mantle without staring at the sepia-toned photographs of the family in happier times.

With a knot in her stomach Olivia began somewhat tensely.

"Papa . . . I have some papers here to show you."

She'd planned on keeping the law school application and its accompanying acceptance letter for last but her nervous hands slipped and those papers slid across the long table before she had a chance to grab them.

She would never forget the stunned reaction of her father as his eyes scanned the papers. And she would never forget how his face changed. He was always a pleasant man with a smile from ear to ear for everyone (except Marco) but now his eyes had fire in them and his smile had turned into a grimace. When he spoke his voice had a cold edge to it. He became louder and louder.

"You're not going, NOT GOING, NOT GOING, to law school. You had NO DAMN BUSINESS EVEN APPLYING."

He continued for several minutes repeating over and over that her place was working at the Inn. None of the women in their family had spent as many years in school and she had. Finally thinking that their talk was over, he gave his last statement on the subject.

"I'm not going to foot the bill FOR ANYMORE CLASSES AND THAT'S THAT."

"Papa . . . I'm being awarded a wonderful grant because of my grades and my entrance test you won't . . ." Her voice trailed off as her father screamed.

"I don't give a damn how many grants you're getting, you're not going." As an afterthought he added, "YOU'RE STAYING RIGHT HERE! Do you understand what I'm saying? YOU'RE NOT GOING ANYWHERE."

In spite of how forceful he sounded Olivia hadn't reached the point of accepting his decision yet. In what she believed would be a last ditch effort, she gathered up the papers and neatly positioned them in a folder in front of him.

"Please Papa . . . please, will you just look through this folder, I'll just leave it here for you."

And with that the discussion came to an abrupt end.

When Olivia got to her room she flopped on her bed in tears. It was where Clarita found her. They talked for hours on what had transpired between

Olivia and their father before Clarita could bring herself to tell her younger sister about Marco.

"Marco's been in a bit of trouble, Liv."

Holding her sister close and as delicately as she could she began a long litany of Marco's wrong doings. Feeling that it would be better if Olivia heard everything from her, Clarita didn't leave out any of the messy details. She gave Olivia the particulars about the English widow, the fashion model and the cocaine.

"Liv, he's just no good, you'll find some great guy someday and be a happily married wife and a happily married attorney too."

Olivia didn't think she had any more tears to shed but with that last remark she broke down again. The two sisters held each other for what seemed an eternity.

After a fitful sleep Olivia awoke to the sound of a heated discussion downstairs. She struggled out of bed and with her ear to the door heard Clarita's voice rising.

"Papa, the Inn is fine for me, I'm happy doing what I'm doing, but it's not what Liv wants. It's just not for her."

After some fiery words the house turned silent and Olivia was left with her thoughts. She tiptoed down to the dining room and her heart sank. The folder, that precious folder was just as she'd left it. Her father hadn't even bothered to open it. Oh, well, she thought, maybe he'll take time tonight to go through it.

Olivia had always been renewed when she went to the beach and that was were she was heading now. Finding an isolated spot she dug her feet into the black sand and watched the waves lazily lapping the shore. She laid back and watched the perfect blue sky washed clean of all but a few wispy clouds and wondered how everything could have gone so wrong. Her dream for the future was withering and the faith she'd had in herself was fading. Maybe she'd never get back to Barcelona. Maybe she'd just stay in San Sebastian and work at the Inn for the rest of her life.

She kept an eye on the waves and thought of all the great times Marco and her had had swimming and sunning. It was then that the thought came to her as if in a bolt of lightening. She had to see him one more time. She'd never been inside the San Sebastian jail but her family was well known in the city and she had no trepidation about requesting a pass to visit Marco. After inquiring, "does your father really know you're here?" and accepting her nod the officer led her to a room with a long table and a long plexiglas divider that ran between prisoner and visitor.

Marco, overjoyed to see her lost no time in trying to set things straight.

"You gotta believe me. The English gal meant nothing to me. It was just a fling, we were just having a little fun."

Noticing Olivia's frown he added, "I was just playing around with her to keep me from missing you so much."

When asked about the fashion model, he stumbled through his answer.

"Well, yes . . . I stayed at her villa but it was just a few times and you gotta believe me . . . nothing ever happened between us. It sure was some beautiful place. Something like the place we'll have someday."

Olivia ignored his last remark and asked about Gina.

Marco felt more and more that he was on a slippery slope. Apparently Olivia had heard more than he thought. He took a deep breath and sheepishly began.

"Well, I guess I got in a little trouble there. But hear me out on this. I was just a little high and I forgot who I was with."

Olivia didn't join him as he laughed.

"Anyway she and her mother are leaving for a clinic in Madrid in a few days and that whole mess will be over with."

Olivia starred at this stranger. He had been the man she'd loved, the man she'd planned to marry, now she couldn't stand the sight of him. She stood up and turned toward the door but not before hurling back one last remark at Marco.

"Marco, you're nothing but a pig."

To clear her head Olivia walked aimlessly for hours before finding herself in front of the Inn. As she eyed the patrons entering and leaving, thoughts of spending the rest of her life working there caused shivers up and down her spine. For the young girl, the future looked very bleak. Every morning she'd check the folder on the dining room table and notice that it hadn't even been opened. And every morning she felt worse than the day before. By now she was feeling the pull of the university and anxious to get on with her new classes. Some days she toyed with the idea of just leaving for Barcelona and never coming back. But then she realized that idea was not an option. Her father would never forgive her, and she would never forgive herself.

Clarita could stand the tension no longer. One late afternoon she headed for the beach and found Olivia starring out to sea. As the two girls strolled along the water's edge, Clarita casually mentioned a very important phone call she'd made the previous evening.

"Cheer up Liv, trust me, soon everything will be worked out, you'll see. I have a plan."

She gave her sister a hug and turned toward the Inn. Olivia couldn't have known that at that very moment a car was speeding away from Madrid and heading north and slightly eastward. A middle-aged exquisitely dressed woman with alert dark eyes and coal black hair touched with wisps of gray was heading for San Sebastian. Aunt Mag was still fuming over the news

Clarita had shared with her the previous evening. How could Eduardo be such a hardheaded lout, she wondered. Oh, well, she reasoned, she hadn't liked him when he married her sister Maria and she certainly didn't like him now. Obviously there was more here than meets the eye.

Her brother-in-law was always stuffing women and their lives into a box that he'd fashioned. He had long since decided that Clarita would be the Pastry Chief, he had his eye on a couple of his older nieces who under his tutelage were learning the fine points of becoming efficient and pleasant waitresses. Other young nieces were following his life's plan and laboring at various kitchen stations. And of course Olivia would be the hostess.

What was the most bothersome to Mag however, was that Eduardo never missed an opportunity to support and encourage the male members of the extended family in whatever career choice they had made. One of his favorite expressions was that education in Spain's best schools and universities "was for men." Following that thinking he was presently footing the bill for a future accountant, doctor, and for two nephews attending one of Madrid's most fashionable culinary schools. The angrier Mag got the faster she drove and the faster ideas popped into her head on how she would diffuse the situation.

First of all, she'd give Eduardo a few good lectures on helping and assisting his daughter to reach her full potential and since Olivia had the grades and drive to make it through law school he had no right to stop her. Yes, that would do it she decided and thought, "I'll be back in Madrid for the opening of the opera by the end of the week." She had no way of knowing that the whole situation couldn't be diffused in a few days. But then Aunt Mag always had an engaging offhanded way of downplaying a bad situation and she was never without a healthy dose of self-confidence. She couldn't have known that the situation between Olivia and her father was worsening and it was not going to be as easy as she thought to "straighten Eduardo out."

By the time Mag arrived at the Inn after midnight, the place was going strong with happy partygoers. Perhaps that was why her fiery conversation with Eduardo couldn't be heard beyond their booth. For almost an hour Mag and her brother-in-law exchanged less than pleasant remarks. He was completely indifferent to Mag's statement, repeated more than once, that to stop Olivia now would be to devalue all that his daughter had accomplished. Realizing that she was getting nowhere Mag headed for the house and looked for Olivia's folder. She sat at the dining room table and went through it page by page and decided Eduardo was even more of a lout than she'd thought.

As the week wore on the tension swelled. It was either one extreme or the other, everybody talking at once pushing their cause, or complete silence, each family member ignoring the opposing side. However, one morning at breakfast Mag, highly disgusted that the problem hadn't been solved yet and irritated that she had missed the opening of the Madrid opera season (the first time in countless years), announced loud and clear that she was leaving in a few hours with Olivia for Barcelona. Further Olivia could call on her "for any money or any support or any encouragement" she needed until she graduated from law school. If there is such a thing as a decisive moment this was it. All eyes were fashioned on Eduardo and the three women couldn't help but give each other a nudge and a wink as he stormed out the door. Clarita, Mag and Olivia scurried around stuffing the car with their luggage and moved onto the last stages of good-bys. They felt that they had done their best with Eduardo and were not prepared to give that problem any more of their time. However, the day wasn't over yet. Almost ready to head out Mag noticed Eduardo's car coming around the bend in the road and finally coming to a stop behind her car. At first Eduardo had little to say. It wasn't easy for him to accept defeat but considering what had gone before he did his best. He could barely be heard muttering to Olivia that she had his blessing and acting a little embarrassed he stuffed a check into Olivia's handbag and added, "Listen, Olivia, you don't need to call on Aunt Mag for money."

After many hugs and tears, Olivia and Mag headed for Barcelona. It had been a struggle but Olivia's dream hadn't withered after all. As the semesters passed envelopes with money neatly folded inside colorful note cards with words of encouragement arrived from Mag. During a visit Eduardo noticed the familiar handwriting on envelopes stacked neatly on Olivia's desk and not to be outdone immediately paid Olivia's tuition for the remaining two years. At Olivia's graduation it was hard to say who was the most proud, student, sister, father or aunt.

Today Olivia is a full-fledged attorney in a prestigious law firm in Madrid and is soon to be married to a handsome and successful banker. She is happy with her life and never forgets the debt she owes her Aunt Mag. While divided by age they are united in their belief that no female should have her choices limited because of gender nor should any female be denied the chance to escape suffocating male domination. Olivia's success is typical of the heights sisters around the world can reach when given a chance.

Chapter Ten

"There is that indescribably freshness and unconsciousness about an illiterate person that humbles and mocks the power of the noblest expressive
genius."

— Walt Whitman

Celia was wide-eyed before the alarm shattered the stillness of the black
night. She had tossed and turned for hours, she was just too excited to sleep.
The same thoughts kept tumbling over and over in her mind. This morning
she'd leave the cramped one room apartment she shared with her parents and
younger sister, Ava and for the first time in her life she'd be in a place where
she'd have enough to eat. She wondered how it would feel to have her own
room and soft bed to sleep in. She felt all grown up when she remembered
that in a few hours she'd begin her job and make money to help her family
who had so little. But special days have a way of falling short of expectations
and while many of the experiences ahead of her would be pleasant, some of
them would teeter on disaster.

Life hadn't been kind to the Diaz family. Celia's father had finally given up
on their tiny plot of ground high in the Peruvian Andes that had been in his
family for generations. The earth was yielding fewer and fewer potatoes each
year and more often than not they had gone to bed feeling empty after a meager supper of scrawny potatoes doused with a hefty supply of hot spices.
Poverty was in the extreme in their settlement and many of the inhabitants
had pondered numerous times leaving the village that they had called home
all their lives. But while they repeatedly hashed over all the advantages of
moving, at the last minute they always seemed to lack the courage to do so.
That changed for Celia's family when two of her uncles carefully tied their

few belongings on the back of a mule, waved good-by and carefully headed down the mountains towards the country's capital, Lima, in search of jobs and a better way of life. Within a few weeks Celia and her family were on their way also.

The trek had hardly been an easy one. They trudged day after day tracking across the mountains' winding trails, watching their feet as they moved ever so carefully along the narrow sloped paths. They skirted tiny villages that looked as humble as the one they had left and journeyed through misty green valleys and past groups of llamas pretending to ignore the small group of strangers, yet eyeing them suspiciously. The travelers crossed footbridges barely a few feet above the unhurried streams snaking off in many directions before spilling into raging rivers. A few nights they slept at the edge of corn-fields and rose with the all-to-rare light of the sun, never complaining instead concentrating on their dreams of the good life that they'd have in Lima. But after three months in the bustling city the good life still seemed to evade them. Perhaps that was why Celia's mother jumped at the chance for her daughter to become a live-in servant in one of Lima's wealthiest families.

Well, the time had come. Celia's father gave her a long tight hug while wiping his eyes and trying to control his voice.

"Don't you ever forget your family."

Her mother also dealing with a volatile mix of emotions handed Celia her frayed satchel, pushed her towards the door, all the while attempting to make light of a tear spilling down her face. Suddenly she broke into a smile that stretched from ear to ear.

"You're going to make lots of money, you'll see." And then as if it was an afterthought she added, "make us proud."

Then the door closed behind her and Celia waited for the van that would take her to her new life. Juan, the driver barely acknowledged the young girl as he half-heartedly thumbed through her papers before flinging her satchel onto a back seat. They raced along recklessly following the main road that cut across the face of the city and then headed south to one of Lima's most elegant suburbs, Miraflores. Celia wondered how he knew when to twist and turn in light of the heavy ghostly fog that had draped itself across the city. Suddenly they reached an opening in the road and waited as large iron gates inched open and they entered the grounds of a stately mansion with lights illuminating its splendor from four sides. Celia had now entered a culture of abundance and opulence.

A side door of the mansion flew open and Celia came face to face with Yolonda who would become her mentor and at times, her witch. She was a big-boned plump woman whose frame gave notice that eating was one of her most enjoyed past times but she still carried herself with a certain grace. Her long coal-black hair with a few strands of gray was piled atop her head and her olive skin told of Spanish ancestors. Her smile appeared forced and when she spoke her words had a certain edginess to them. When she circled Celia her piercing dark eyes noted every detail of the frightened young girl. Then as if speaking to someone else in the room she pronounced Celia's arms and legs "ample and strong." Celia stood on one foot and shifted her weight to the other as Yolonda began her litany of rules.

There would be no time for idleness. In the morning she would be expected in the kitchen at 5 A.M. to assist with breakfast after which the silver was to be washed and polished to a glittering shine. The rooms were to be vacuumed every morning, all rooms were to be dusted every day and all bed lines changed daily. She would then present herself back in the kitchen in late morning to help with the main meal at noon. In the afternoon she was to finish the laundry and prepare for a light meal in the evenings. Yolonda stopped for a split second inquiring, "do you understand?" However, before Celia had time to nod "yes" Yolonda picked up where she'd left off. Celia was to speak only if she was spoken to. She would give a slight curtsy whenever she met Señor and Señora Alvereze and the Grande Dame Josefina.

At thirteen years of age, well almost fourteen she would proudly tell you, Celia was about to come upon things she never thought existed. Her tour began in the Grand Hall, rich with tapestries. Handsomely carved cherry mahogany cabinets lined the wide corridor and held plaques and trophies of polo matches in Chile, Argentina and, and world wide yacht races. The Reception Room had windows that ran from the floor to the lofty ceiling covered with rich red velvet draperies held in place with thick golden tassels. The room was filled with overstuffed chairs, sofas and brushed wood tables with ornate lamps that were to "remain on all the time." The ivory colored Banquet Room where Celia eventually would be serving was fitted with gilded paneling. A massive sparkling crystal chandelier with hundreds of teardrop prisms hung gracefully from the elaborately painted sky blue ceiling overhead. The size of the long oak table gave evidence of many formal dinners and was topped with a large elaborately embroidered linen tablecloth. Fragile gold and crimson table settings were properly placed among the exquisite sparkling crystal. The downstairs tour ended when Yolonda took Celia to her room in a detached building a short distance from the back of the house. Her last words to Celia were particularly scathing.

"You're to throw those old tattered shoes out and fix your hair for god's sake. Get rid of that one long braid down your back. Remember you are no longer living like you used to and you are to act accordingly. She reached for Celia's satchel and added, "this is a disgrace, throw it out. We don't have junk like that around here. And, one more thing, I will check your room periodically. It is to be kept clean and tidy at all times." Yolonda turned to leave and then stopped for a second. With her hand on the doorknob she added, "remember what I have said. And by the way, thievery is a cause of immediate dismissal."

Celia stood transfixed as her eyes covered the room. So what if the room was hardly bigger than a closet. So what if the bathroom actually was a closet. So what if the bed was extremely narrow. So what if the one piece of shabby furniture was a chest with only had two small drawers that at times refused to open. She didn't have many clothes anyway. For the first time in her life she had her own room and that was good. Everything was good she told herself. However, beneath her innocence and in spite of her excitement over her new job, an anxiety was growing deep inside her. Still, she couldn't have known that in some respects her new life would be harsher than the one she'd left.

When she'd think back on it she'd remember that her first afternoon was little more than a blur. She combed and brushed her hair over and over and somewhat successfully fashioned it neatly in curls on top of her head. Still she felt she looked funny. She attempted to break in a pair of new black shiny shoes that were uncomfortable and she considered ugly and she donned her gray-blue uniform with its stiff white cuffs and collar. She then made her way to the kitchen where the cook was waiting impatiently for her. The huge room housed three glistening white gas ranges beside two oversized white refrigerators next to a massive tall freezer. An immense gray stone fireplace took up one end of the room. On the west wall several tall windows let in the afternoon sun and in spite of its size, the room appeared to have a homey and cheerful atmosphere. The day servants were in their assigned places doing their assigned tasks and so the only sound was the noise of utensils at work. Everyone seemed to be caught up in a flurry of activity preparing for a special early afternoon luncheon with numerous guests. It would be one of the many luncheons and banquets held in the lavish house and cause Celia to break out in a cold sweat. While she was at the bottom of the totem pole still no matter what chore she was given she seemed to fall short of what was expected of her and no matter what she did or where she stood she could feel Yolonda's piercing eyes on her. Somehow she got through her first day and when she was dismissed she fled to the peace and safety of her tiny room to collapse on her bed in tears.

The days blended into weeks and Celia bit by bit began to be a little more comfortable in her routine. She learned to work faster, indeed many days she appeared to be running instead of walking while moving through the house. She prepared trays in the kitchen but hated moving into the Banquet Room to serve guests. She learned to work well into the night in the kitchen after a special event and be back on her toes before dawn. By trial and error she discovered what particular chores her mentor would check and if pressed for time, as she usually was, she knew what she could leave until the following morning. But perhaps most of all she learned how to hold back the tears at Yolonda's smarting criticism that occurred at regular intervals. Some nights Celia wondered if Yolonda was indeed a witch as some of the day servants had nicknamed her.

Celia eventually met Señor Alvereze, a tall man with thick gray hair and deep set brown eyes. He was the owner of numerous mining companies and other flourishing Peruvian business ventures. Señora Alvereze, a pretty woman was always dressed to perfection and always in a rush to leave in the morning. She was a successful attorney and a partner of one of the country's leading law firms. The couple had a daughter, Margarita, known affectionately as "Mar," who was in school in Switzerland and of whom they often spoke.

When Celia caught sight of the couple sitting together on one of the oversized sofas and holding hands after dinner she couldn't help but daydream that someday she'd have a marriage just like they had. She thought of her parents and realized that they barely acknowledged each other. They were too busy just trying to survive, thus romance and tenderness was the last thing on their minds. Celia also met the Grande Dame Josefina, the Señor's mother. A small white-haired lady, with a quick smile, she was the epitome of the affluent Peruvian matron. She'd dedicated her life to various charitable causes and was always searching for a new challenge. She now found life boring and dull as she recovered from hip replacement surgery.

The second floor bedrooms were beautifully furnished with massive chests and wardrobes. Huge beds sat in the middle of the large rooms topped with soft comforts and numerous floppy pillows. Ornate mirrors highlighted the walls covered with delicately embossed wallpaper. Celia couldn't help but chuckle to herself when she saw the elaborate gold spigots in the bathrooms. At home one rusty old spigot, if it was a "good water day" would provide water for six, seven families or more.

While all of it was breath taking, it was a small room off the Grande Dame Josefina's bedroom that held a special fascination for Celia. The door, fitted with a tiny stained glass window, was always locked and she'd been forbidden to open it or step inside. Still at thirteen (almost fourteen) she still had the curiosity of a small child. One afternoon as she was finishing vacuuming Josefina's bedroom she spied a small bronze key on the dresser and wondered if it could be the key to that forbidden room she had so often passed. Unable to resist the impulse she quietly made her way to the door, slipped the key in the lock and turned the elaborate doorknob. Nothing could have prepared her for what was inside.

The room was in total darkness except for a few flickering red votive candles on a small altar that held a heavy brushed gold crucifix. Celia counted three pews with kneelers and in some way the room reminded her of the country church she had visited as a little girl a half-days walk from her old village. As her eyes slowly adjusted to the darkness she noticed a small jewel encrusted table with a mosaic top standing by the side of the altar. On the wall above the table two swords hanging in their sheaths were surrounded by the family's coat of arms. Other armorial artifacts gave evidence of a long proud family. But while everything in the little room had a disquieting beauty to it, it was what was on the table that set Celia's heart pounding. It was a book. She couldn't have known that the prayer book was a treasured antique that had been presented to the family by the Vatican centuries earlier.

The sound of Yolonda's heels clicking on the highly polished mahogany parquet floor brought Celia back to reality. In a split second she had the door closed and locked. She then rushed to deposit the key where she'd found it. But while she followed her usual afternoon routine her thoughts were of the unusual room and the unusual book. She fell asleep that night and many nights to come thinking of the few times she had held a book in her hands and had scanned all its wonderful pictures.

Celia's schooling had been on a hit and miss basis. More often than not she had no shoes to walk to the one room schoolhouse across a small ravine near her parent's hut. Unfortunately more often than not, a teacher would stay for a few short weeks and then move on leaving the village children with only bits of lessons. While the other children were contented with the haphazard arrangement Celia would be in tears watching the teacher pack up, climb on an old donkey and wave good-by. At thirteen (almost fourteen) Celia was unable to read. More than once her father had tried to soothe her.

"You don't need to read. Someday you'll be a woman, married and have lots of babies to take care of . . . women don't need to learn to read . . . look at your mother. She can't read. You just try to be a good wife and mother someday . . . that's all you need to know."

With this background it is easy to see the fascination the book held for Celia. It was on her mind while she cleaned and scrubbed, dusted and vacuumed and whenever she could she'd escape into the little room, reach for the book and for a few precious moments strain her eyes to capture every image as she carefully turned the pages. One afternoon, so deeply enthralled with what she was doing, she didn't notice that the door behind her was slightly ajar. Nor did she notice the sound of footsteps coming closer, ever closer. At the last minute Celia in a panic took the book, hid it inside her uniform and dropped to the floor behind a pew. She recognized the voice, "now why is this door opened?" It was Yolonda. Celia prayed she couldn't hear the pounding of her heart. Yolonda gave the room a quick scan and unable to notice the terror stricken young girl in the semi-darkness, closed and locked the door. If Celia had not been in a panic, she would never have made her blunder.

The young girl was almost to her room when she realized she still had the book hidden in her uniform. She checked her clock. It was too late to return the book now, it was almost time to assist the cook preparing the evening meal. She did the only thing she could do under the circumstances. She gently deposited the book in her dresser drawer and headed for the kitchen. She didn't know that outrage about the missing book was already flowing through the house.

Just as Celia was finishing her evening kitchen work, Yolonda, burst into the room. Suddenly she reached out and grabbed Celia's arm. Her eyes had fire in them and her voice was cold and determined.

"You are to present yourself to Sēnor Alvereze immediately."

The young girl already could hear muffled noises seeping into the kitchen and with some trepidation she pushed the door open and came face to face with the family.

The questioning began at a rapid-fire pace. Did she know the rules about the chapel? Had she ever gone into the chapel? Limited in her scope of experiences at first she shook her head "no" to everything. Suddenly Yolonda triumphantly entered the inquisition room with the precious book in her hand and jubilantly announced exactly where she'd found it. Celia felt as if she was sliding into a deep black hole and the hole was getting bigger and bigger with no hope of escape.

The room was shocked into silence. All eyes glared at Celia. Once too shy to barely speak to the Señor, Señora and the Grande Dame, the frightened young girl blurted out a few sentences.

"I can't read. And, well, I though . . . I thought that I . . . could learn to read from the book."

She was unsuccessful in her effort to hold back her tears. The next few minutes were a complete blur and finally she was dismissed and she fled to the safety of her room.

Yolonda was only a few steps behind her. Her voice was unusually shrill as she embarked on a tirade. She was an ungrateful girl. She hadn't appreciated her job. Now she'd pay the consequences of her thievery. She was to get ready to go home and never come back. Between sobs Celia packed the few pieces of clothing she had and prepared for the worst. When finished she paced the floor feeling more terror stricken than she had ever been. Back and forth she stepped with thoughts darting through her head. What would become of her now? What if she never found another job? What would her parents think of her? For most of the night she paced and cried and thought. She had no way of knowing that the family had shook their heads at the incident, told Yolonda to "handle it," and scattered to various rooms to follow their own endeavors.

Yolonda was on a mission to find Juan to deposit the wanton girl "back where she belonged." Fortunately Juan assuming he was not needed for the evening became friendly with a large bottle of Pisco. Drinking the sour grape brandy was his favorite pastime and as the evening passed he became more and more incoherent. By the time Yolonda flung open his door he was totally and completely drunk, much to her chagrin.

Señor Alvereze had retired to the library to study some profit and loss statements, the Señora was in the upstairs study reworking some briefs for an important court case scheduled for the next morning. The Grande Dame Josefina was in her bedroom, pacing back and forth as thoughts rumbled through her head. What would happen to the young girl? She wasn't more than a child and all she wanted was to learn to read. Now she was going to be flung out into society where the gap between the rich and the poor never seemed to lesson. How many other young girls were mired in illiteracy, forced to go through life without basic skills in reading and writing and worst of all with no hope of a better life? It was almost dawn when Josefina stopped her soul searching and stopped her pacing. She knew what she had to do. It was time she reasoned to make herself useful, really useful. It was one thing to be a fund-raiser and be removed a step or two from the cause and another thing to have hands-on where it was needed the most. She'd face some resistance she knew that, but she had made up her mind and that would be that.

Assuming she'd have to leave soon, Celia pulled her shabby shawl closer, reached for her worn satchel that she'd refused to throw out and slowly ambled along the pathway to the main house. Wondering how "the poor girl was doing" the Grande Dame marched along the pathway to the servant quarters. Celia was wondering why the Grande Dame was coming towards her and Josefina was wondering why Celia was out of uniform and carrying her satchel. Can you imagine the immediacy of a moment like that?

The two sat on a bench in the garden and talked and at times fell silent just listening to the sound of water gurgling from one of the gardens many stone fountains. Celia couldn't believe her ears. She was reprimanded for her deed, of course, but there was more. The elderly woman took Celia's hand.

"You will learn to read and write, I promise you that."

Yolonda would receive orders that Celia was to be given an hour off three times a week for tutoring. The talk was over but the Grande Dame couldn't resist adding a footnote.

"It's time Yolonda learned who is boss around her."

The next few weeks things happened at break neck speed. Without any fanfare a room in the guest house was renovated and desks along with blackboards, caulk and books arrived. Josefina was sprier that ever using her connections to reach a few other young women who as generations before them had done, accepted the status quo without question. Eventually to everyone's pleasant surprise the little classroom was filled to capacity. Well, that is almost everyone was pleased.

Celia had a new round of doubts. What if she couldn't learn to read? What if the others were smarter than she was? What if they laughed at her and called her dummy? Would she ever catch up to other girls her age? She didn't need to worry. Within a few months she was looking forward to the challenge of each new lesson and it wasn't long before she was ahead of the curve. She was being introduced to a new feeling, something she'd never felt before, pride in herself.

Now for the first time in her life Celia toys with the idea of secondary school and maybe even attending college and she revels in the joy of that thought. She feels a sense of accomplishment that due to her coaxing and cajoling her mother and little sister Ava, now attend classes regularly.

The Grande Dame Josefina feels as if she'd had an epiphany. She doesn't want any accolades, the joy that the little classroom brings her, the fulfillment she feels as each girl advances mean more to her than her honorary old world title and all the luxuries she enjoys. Some of her wealthy women friends seeing the need have reserved some of their own time or hired retired teachers to educate their staff in basic reading and writing.

Josefina began with one frightened illiterate girl and together they have shown that given the opportunity women from both sides of the tracks can work together. Celia and her cohorts now feel that life can be a changeable structure of possibilities and that it indeed can be bright with promise and they hope that their example will become a beacon to other women in similar situations. United in their efforts to help each other and to better themselves, they too are part of the global sisterhood.

Chapter Eleven

"Although the world is full of suffering, it is full also of the overcoming of it."

—Helen Keller

Nina awoke to the wonderful sound of water gushing through the pipes, which meant that the plumbing had been repaired once again. The past week had been a struggle. For five days the worn and rusty pipes and spigots had creaked and groaned to push water as far as the seventh floor. Unfortunately Nina lived on the eighth floor and through trial and error had learned to make due with a trickle of water for her needs.

Things always seemed to be breaking down in the dismal no-frills apartment buildings. Several years earlier they had been constructed by the government for poor city dwellers and peasants who'd been forced to leave their beloved land and move to urban areas where they could more easily be spied upon. But while life was better since the country was out from under the heel of Communism much still had to be done to rectify the bad management and corruption Romanians had endured under the reign of Dictator Nicolae Ceausescu.

While Nina's friends and coworkers were confident that their lives would continue to improve, some days it was hard not to be deeply discouraged especially the mornings when the lines of the unemployed seemed endless. The country was making a slow and tenuous march toward a market economy and Nina was fortunate to be working at the General Jobs Exchange supplying the few new businesses and various struggling industries with personnel. The pay was minimal but the real reward was watching the smiles sweep across the faces of the men and women she had connected to jobs.

Many of them were living in abysmal poverty but still clung to Clug-Napoca, a busy university city and one of Romania's main economic centers with a population of over 300,000. Others, the victims of Ceausescu's reset-tlement policies that had played havoc with their lives, used their newfound freedom to make the trek back to their homes in the renewed hope that their houses and small barns were still intact. Unfortunately once there they dis-covered that the government had bulldozed their settlements. Thus many were left with nothing more than empty fields and for them the life of a peas-ant farmer had lost its allure. Discouraged and disheartened they retraced their steps back to the city in the hope of finding employment and a better life.

Nina hoped that her mother, Anna would follow their example but so far she stubbornly avoided any talk of pulling up roots and moving in with her daughter. Anna was living in one of the small picturesque Fagaras Mountain cities where her family had lived for hundreds of years. She had married, pro-duced three children and buried her husband, Mircea. Well known in the com-munity, Mircea could not adapt himself to the requirements of the Commu-nist regime. He had been picked up by the Securitate and made an example of. His crime was writing and discussing the numerous social ills that com-munism had created. Anna was left with three children to raise and supported her family with her job in one of the country's best health spas.

For the most part the area had remained unchanged. Indeed during the height of Communism the slopes had seen many government officials arriv-ing with their entourages of minions to visit the spas or the peaks, skiing, hik-ing and ice-skating. Now the few Romanian citizens who could afford a few days holiday were once again returning to the mountains free of the dreaded secret police and the area was attempting a slow return to minimal prosperity.

Perhaps that was why Nina's heart skipped a beat when she tore open her mother's curt letter instructing her to return home as soon as possible. At first reading Nina was stricken with the urgency it seemed to convey but always optimistic she seized on the idea that her mother must have some wonderful news to share with her. Maybe it was a special family reunion to say good-by to her brother Ilie who having reached age eighteen was obliged to enter the military. Maybe it was a wedding for her sister Daniela. At any rate, Nina de-cided it had to be something special and following her mother's command be-gan her journey. How could she have known that what she'd soon face would change her life and her mother's life forever.

As she merged into the crowd at the train station she couldn't help but re-count the country's many changes. Romanians for some years now were en-joying their freedom to watch and to listen to the country's diverse television and radio stations, some less than ten years old. As she waited to board the train her eyes darted across her fellow passengers. Everyone was deeply involved reading the independent newspapers and periodicals. It was almost as if the whole country couldn't stop making up for lost time with every free moment devoted to reading their rich and diverse press that had been denied them so long under the Communists.

It was the same when she settled into her seat and the train began its journey to Brasov, Transylvania's largest city. She watched as many of the passengers were pleasantly trading their reading materials and she was delighted to share a newspaper with a young woman next to her. On the front page the bold headlines seemed to jump out.

"NEW WORRIES AS AIDS SWEEPS THE COUNTRY."

Underneath, statistics from a World Health Organization study indicated that many of those afflicted with the disease were in their teens. The click clack of the train lured Nina to sleep before she had time to finish the article and when she awoke the bright light of the sun was reflecting off the compartment's window. At Brasov she found her luggage and moved through the somewhat busy terminal searching for her brother Ilie.

As she waited for him her mind floated back to the early years. Her baby brother Ilie and younger sister Daniela had always tagged after her and the three of them had spent many happy moments near the craggy summits and the pointed peaks watching the abundant wild life that always seemed to encircle the area in springtime. Many afternoons were spent lying in the soft warm grass near massive old trees and eyeing the branches teeming with hundreds of chirping birds. Oh, how they had laughed as they watched the black goats scampering about on the nearby hills. Winters were a wonderland of snow and ice skating on a nearby glacier lake. The three of them would spend hours gliding over the slick ice creating new moves, showing off their twirls along with the town's other children.

While the adults were less than pleased with the heavy snows that completely buried their houses and the back-breaking work it took to dig out, the children delighted in climbing through the snowdrifts to watch the smoke rise from what otherwise appeared to be just a huge mound of snow. It didn't seem possible how fast the years had slipped by. Both Ilie and Daniela were pre-teens when Nina left home to continue her education. Soon Daniela would complete high school and follow in her sister's footsteps and attend the university in Cluj. Nina's thoughts lingered on her sister. She had to be the prettiest girl in her class. Her deep brown eyes seemed to enhance her long flowing auburn hair that she had taken so much pride in since she was a little girl. Nina chuckled as she remembered her sister constantly brushing her long locks with the result that its beautiful sheen only added to her attractiveness.

Nina, didn't have long to wait to greet Ilie. It would be a few minutes before she realized that her brother, always engaged in good- natured teasing, was now completely serious and tightlipped. No amount of her prodding questions about their mother or sister was greeted with a straight answer, instead "you'll see" remained his pat reply and for the remainder of the journey they were silent. What Nina would see this day would linger in her mind forever.

Daniela was resting in bed with Anna hovering over her. The once pretty and healthy girl was now reduced to little more than a skeleton. For the past several weeks the young girl had been continually losing weight and had no interest in eating even the semolina with sugar water prepared by Anna, an ancient remedy given for most afflictions. Daniela spent most of her time lying flat in bed, too weak to even sit-up. Her skin had a pale, ashen look and her once beautiful hair had lost its sheen and remained dull and lifeless. The initial diagnoses had been pneumonia from a local doctor but it was clear that there was something else going on in Daniela's body. The next morning they lifted her gently into Ilie's car, fixed her as comfortable as possible and made the trip to a large hospital in Brasov. For days they sat and dozed by Daniela's bed and watched her deteriorate even further. No amount of medicine seemed to lessen her high fever. Finally one gray dismal morning a group of doctors came in with startling news and addressed Anna.

"Mrs. Vlahuta, your daughter. . . we may not be able to save her from the pneumonia. . . you see, her blood work indicates she has AIDS."

That twenty-four-word sentence was always with them, during the endless days, during the long tiring nights as they lingered by the once beautiful young girl's bedside. Then one quiet afternoon when the hospital seemed unusually peaceful Daniela awoke from her semi-stupor and appeared strangely alert. Her eyes took on a frenzied look as she lifted her thin arm and motioned for Nina to come closer. While every word seemed to be a struggle she told Nina she'd had a vision from "the angels in heaven." Between fits of coughing and in a muffled voice she told Nina that the angels were waiting for her.

"Tell Mama I'm sorry. I'm sorry. Oh, I'm so sorry."

Nina leaned over and answered.

"Daniela, she'll be back in a few minutes and you can tell her yourself. You'll be all better soon."

"No, I'm going to die."

A tranquil look flushed across the sick girl's pale face as she drifted into semi-consciousness. Nina wondered what Daniela had to be so sorry about. Perhaps it was just the fever and the drugs talking and she decided to dismiss the subject. She couldn't of course. It just lay there in the back of her mind, emerging and nagging and receding without warning.

The sick young teenager lingered the rest of the week but on a cold somber night she floated away and Anna, Nina and Ilie were left to deal with their sorrow. Returning to their small mountain city they climbed the old stone steps of the church and watched as Daniela's casket was slowly placed near the altar. After the service heavy with holy incense she was laid next to her father not far from a lazy stream rapidly freezing as the temperatures fell. Mother, son and daughter lingered awhile at the gravesite each lost in their own thoughts and unable to pull themselves away not just yet. Suddenly something dawned on all three of them about the same time!

None of their relatives or friends had made the journey to the hospital in Brasov, which Nina and Anna had brushed off not as a lack of love and affection but rather because of the distance. But none of their relatives or friends had come by the house to visit or comfort and none had attended Daniela's church services. No one followed the slow gate of the horse pulling a dilapidated wagon carrying the casket save Anna, Nina, Ilie and the parish priest. It had always been the custom that the townspeople joined the family of the deceased in the slow sad trek to the cemetery whether one knew them well or not. How strange that Daniela's funeral would break that long held community custom.

The next morning Anna's supervisor banged on the door. He was politely hostile and didn't mince any words. Anna now was a determent to the health spa, they would lose customers when they heard about her daughter. At first Anna was too stunned to answer but then she found her voice.

"My daughter died of pneumonia, how could that be bad for the spa?"

When he answered everything seemed to come clear, the bare church, the lack of people at the cemetery, the house empty of relatives and friends.

"Anna, there are rumors floating around that your daughter died of AIDS and people are afraid. We just don't want to be near any of you."

The next few days were nothing short of agony. Ilie left for the military after many tears and good-byes. Anna felt she was now losing a son and was totally devastated. She wouldn't speak of the AIDS that had claimed her youngest daughter's life. She was convinced that it was pneumonia and nothing more that took Daniela from her. Nina burst into tears every time she passed the old highchair in the cellar where her sister had wiggled and squirmed so many years ago.

One afternoon as the dense clouds floated overhead promising a flake or two of snow, Nina and Anna began their daily trek down an old narrow road with more than its share of potholes. At the cemetery they pulled their mufflers closer and sat beside the freshly covered grave. Even though Nina felt uneasy asking, she had to know.

"Moma, what happened between you and Daniela?"

There was a long unnerving pause and finally Anna stared at the ground, took a deep breath and spoke of the turmoil they had lived through for the past few years. Daniela had gone through a rebellious time. No matter what they talked about, their conversations always seemed to curl into an endless round of accusations. Anna was "just too old-fashioned;" Daniela was "a disobedient girl behaving badly" and on and on.

The truth was that the young girl was traveling with a wild crowd who cared little for school. Many of them cut classes and had been found drunk in the middle of the day. Anna's rules about staying out late were meaningless. Many of the teenagers had tired of their monotonous life in the small mountain city and decided to run away, confident of a better time in Bucharest. One evening Anna came home from work and found a short note.

"Mama, don't worry. Love Daniela."

Anna felt her daughter would get over her wanderlust and return and when Daniela did come back several months later, she felt as if she had handled the situation well.

The grieving mother began to talk non-stop. It was as if a floodgate had opened on what she had been holding inside for so long. She tried to get her daughter to return to school but the young girl would have none of it. Daniela always had enjoyed her classes and sports and choir but now she was lethargic with little interest in anything. She spent most of her days in bed, yet she was always tired. Anna made one of her favorite dishes, mititei, and when the young girl couldn't keep the meat down, Anna fixed supa but even the noodles couldn't wet the sick girl's appetite. She was getting sicker and sicker and the inghetata that Anna purchased at a local ice cream shop was the only food she could handle.

The days melted into weeks and all Daniela wanted was to be left alone to sleep. The little time she was awake, mother and daughter argued about returning to school, giving up her friends and going to a doctor.

"Nina, your sister was a good girl, she just got mixed up with the wrong people."

Nina held her mother close and answered in a low whisper.

"Mama you must face what Daniela died from. It was AIDS because of unprotected sex or maybe she was doing drugs with dirty needles."

Anna's face went white and she burst out in anger.

"How dare you say that of your own sister. It was pneumonia I tell you."

"Moma, don't turn your back on the truth. It's because people don't know enough about the disease that it's spreading all over the country—even the whole damn world."

Anna wouldn't be dissuaded and exploded.

"It was pneumonia! Now I don't want to hear another word about it."

They walked back to the house in silence holding their thoughts tightly to themselves. The remainder of the evening no one spoke and anguish filled the small house.

As the days went on Nina was caught between her obligation to her mother and helping her to get through the sorrow and yet being fearful of losing her job if she didn't return to Cluj soon. No amount of cajoling, persuading and pleading could get Anna to accompany her. They bid a tension-ridden good-bye and with promises of "I'll write soon" Nina was on her way. The scene would remain with her, Anna lingering in the doorway, sad, dejected and with misty eyes. What would become of her, Nina wondered. The townspeople had been so cruel, they couldn't get past their preconceived notions about AIDS. Nina didn't share her mother's belief that the callous treatment from the townspeople would soon fade away.

As time moved on no matter what else occupied Nina's mind she continued to worry about Anna. She lived for her mother's weekly notes even though they provided little news. Anna conveniently "forgot" to reveal that she continued to be an outcast in the community. When she headed downtown the townspeople dropped their eyes and crossed the street so as not to pass her. When she entered the market it seemed as if the aisles emptied immediately and church services were no different, she sat alone. Nor did Anna mention that she was rapidly going through her little box of money that had always rested safely in the cellar's rafters. It had been added to and subtracted from more times than she could remember during the years. She'd called it her "emergency reserve money."

It was inevitable that the day would arrive when Anna would have to make a decision to leave the town or continue to endure the inevitable heartache of being shunned by her relatives and her old friends. At first she dismissed the idea of moving to Cluj. She'd always had a special feeling for her home and her garden which had kept them alive during the hard times. How could she ever leave a lifetime of memories behind? Yet fear washed over her. How much longer could she survive emotionally and financially without a job? Her fears ricochet through her mind all day and during her many sleepless nights. By the time Ilie came home on furlough she was still vacillating about leaving.

It didn't take long for Ilie to size up the situation and see that something had to be done quickly to help his mother. Remembering that she had always fiercely resisted being pressured, late one afternoon he nonchalantly spoke of driving up to Cluj to see Nina for a few days.

"Say Moma, think you'd like to come along? Just for a few days?"

Anna, with little else to occupy her time gave him a halfhearted nod "yes." How could they have known that an opportunity would present itself and change Anna's life more that any of them had ever imagined?

The trip was pleasant. Anna was proud of her son. He looked so handsome with his new mandatory haircut and neatly pressed military uniform. They chatted pleasantly about his training and his hopes of a long successful military career but Anna ignored his bitter remarks about their hometown as well as the information he had gained from an AIDS awareness class on base. She remained quiet and stared at the passing fields that had at one time produced crops, now they were nothing more than dusty patches of withering grass and weeds.

While mother and son were heading north to Cluj an interesting personnel request came across Nina's desk. She was usually trying to get employers and tentative employees together in the building trades but this request was far different. Her eyes ran across the paper and she read about a new orphanage ready for occupancy on the outskirts of Tirgu about a six-hour trip south from Cluj. They needed a "warm, loving woman to handle babies, toddlers and older children. Live-in housemother preferred."

Nina's heart raced. This would be perfect for Anna if only she could talk her into it. For the rest of the day she couldn't get her mind off the orphanage. And she couldn't get her mind off her mother. Somehow she had to bring the two together but how? Of course, she had no way of knowing that Anna and Ilie were on their way to see her at that very moment. When she sleepily answered a knock at the door well after midnight Ilie and Anna were standing there as if out of a dream. After many hugs and tears they spent much of the next few hours talking about everything and about nothing in particular. They were just happy to be together once again.

It would be great to say that Anna immediately was agreeable to at least thinking about Nina's job request. She wasn't of course. She had no need to go to an orphanage and repeated it over and over again. Still she was amenable to taking the trip if for no other reason than to pacify her son and daughter. Early one morning just as the sun was barely peeking over the horizon the three of them piled into Ilie's car and headed south and east to the new orphanage at Tirgu

The large unassuming building was nestled in a wooded area a short distance from a narrow zigzagging road. A high-fenced play yard at the back curled around both sides of the building. The sun was dancing across the large entry hall as they entered and met Director Ionica Tzara a large woman with a soft comforting voice and a heartwarming smile. At first the conversation was light hearted and trivial, just a few words about the trip to Tirgu, Ilie's military training and Nina's work in Clug. But as they followed the director through the freshly painted rooms, the conversation took on a somber almost heartbreaking note.

A door opened into an already filled-to-capacity room with cribs housing sleeping or crying babies. In another section with windows from floor to ceiling they watched a caregiver fussing over toddlers. A large room to the back of the building had older children with sad eyes attempting to amuse themselves with balls, wooden trucks, a few dolls and an assortment of other ragtag toys. Through it all Anna remained speechless as she followed a step or two behind the director but her eyes were sweeping back and forth across the children and she realized that all of them were tugging at her heartstrings. Nina's heart skipped a beat when the director casually mentioned that many of the children were orphans because both or one of their parents were dead or dying of AIDS. Still others had begun their short lives as HIV-positive children and had been abandoned by their parents.

Perhaps it was watching Ilie kneeling on the floor and listening intently to a small black-headed boy explaining between sobs how his bright red truck had lost its front wheels. Perhaps it was seeing Nina attempting to soothe a crying baby, or perhaps it was the pull on her sleeve as a small hand folded into her own that caused Anna to realize that she couldn't leave this place and not come back. A few weeks later and after much soul searching Anna moved lock, stock and barrel into the orphanage and thus began a new fulfilling chapter in her life.

She and the staff are never idle from early morning to late at night. But for Anna the most rewarding part of the day happens at dusk when the children are being prepared for bed. The little ones have the routine down pat as they wait their turn to climb onto Anna's lap as she rocks them and sings a soft lullaby, the very lullaby that she had so often sang to Daniela. Many times Anna is overcome with emotion as she wonders what will happen to her little ones. She is well aware that the European Community is presently at odds about what is best for the children. Some urge "in-country" adoptions only while other countries are pressing for international adoptions. Meanwhile the ranks of orphans are growing by leaps and bounds in their country as it is in other parts of the globe.

While the orphanage takes up most of her time, Anna now has discovered the courage to work in tandem with Nina. Mother and daughter have received training and instructions which have enabled them to give talks and hold discussion groups for any organization willing to listen about the HIV/AIDS epidemic sweeping the globe. Working in their respective cities they have access to literature of the Working Group of the World Health Organization (WHO), United Nations Aids (UNAIDS) and other essential national and international institutions who are laboring to educate the public on behavior which can spur transmission of HIV. The frank talks encourage the use of condoms, discarding infected needles, and equally vital, erasing the many misconception people have about the disease. They especially are involved with teenagers and pre-teens because it appears that that age group is the fastest growing group being infected.

Anna now had the courage to speak of her personal tragedy in the earnest hope it will give others the wherewithall to do better when confronted with the disease.

"My daughter died of AIDS and I was in denial. I didn't know because I didn't want to know about AIDS. That was something that happened to other people not someone in my family."

With telephones available at the orphanage and at Nina's office, mother and daughter constantly share their experiences. They have empowered each other. Anna with the help of her family has overcome hurdles that would have defeated one with less inner strength. She along with her daughter are vibrant members of the dedicated women across the planet that realize that one needs to embrace change in order to make the world a better place. As they move ahead they are being joined by others of their gender who labor to solve the critical issues facing not only women but all of humanity.

Chapter Twelve

"Nothing and no one can destroy the Chinese people. They are relentless survivors."

—Pearl Buck

Maya sank into her narrow and uncomfortable pad and as she had managed every night for the past few months she tuned out the chattering of the other women who were milling around nearby. It seemed as if nothing ever changed in their austere and cramped, semi-dark and stuffy sleeping room in one of Shanghai's many multistory dormitory buildings destined to house the city's almost two million factory workers. It was the same every week on the eve of a day off, the other women squatting on the floor counting their small earnings and deciding where to spend their precious day away from their machines.

Perhaps they'd hop on a bus and wind their way through the traffic-choked streets to the city's acclaimed Art Museum or meander through the serene five-acre Yu Gardens. Or maybe they'd linger near one of the many sites where new buildings were springing up to eyeball the workers in the midst of modern equipment still digging out the foundations with picks and shovels. Shanghai was experiencing a colossal building boom as were much of China's major cities and the landscape of the city changed almost daily. But none of this interested Maya, she was always too tired and weary to do anything but arrive before the first light of dawn at her workstation in a large men's shirt factory to begin her grueling sixteen-hour workday.

As Maya turned toward the wall she closed her eyes and dreamt of a different job where she too could count on working only six days a week. But she knew that that wouldn't happen for a few months. In a panic to find a job after she left her home a few hundred miles to the west and slightly south of Shanghai, she'd agreed to work one year at one of the area's almost ten thousand factories producing goods for the overseas market. She had three months to go and she intended to honor her contract even though at times she felt as if she was in jail.

The factory doors were locked as soon as every employee, dressed in their drab blue uniforms, sat at his or her workstation. Talking during the day was forbidden and most of the workers didn't even know the name of the person only a few feet from them. After a short break for a meager lunch and dinner they returned in unison to their stations. Even on the brightest days the workers couldn't catch the sun's rays, the closed and locked windows were completely covered with dust and grime and no matter how hot the weather the air conditioners lay idle unless a government official or foreign entrepreneur was expected. On those days one couldn't help but notice the contrast between the employees' old bikes or scratch and dented scooters parked in a far-off dusty and rutted field and the visitors' sleek Mercedes or highly polished BMW's parked nearby on a cleaned paved lot. The laborers became so used to the roar of the machines that when the sounds stopped at quitting time they still heard the din of the machines in their heads. If a worker complained he or she was immediately fired and several times Maya quickly caught sight of strange new faces nearby anxiously struggling to master their complicated machines.

Working on assigned pieces of men's shirts was monotonous but the workers didn't have time to be bored as almost every week production quotas were raised. Maya started in the button section and spent her days sorting and distributing buttons and trimmings to the various departments. Within two months she had been transferred to one of the sewing sections attaching collars and when she arrived back at the dorm each night her fingers were cracked and bloody but she never complained. Her family was the reason she was in Shanghai and most months when her brother Yugao arrived for her money to buy the needed medicine, she gave him her entire pay, other months she kept a few coins for herself.

Maya thought of her family constantly. Before she left the family's mud and brick hut her mother and father were too weak and fatigued some days to even get out of bed and according to Yugao they seemed to be getting worse. At first no one had given a name to their afflictions or the similar maladies effecting the other village residents but rumor had it that unsafe blood work was the cause of the poor health and numerous deaths devastating the small rural community.

Several years earlier when the settlement still lacked a clinic the government opened a blood station in a nearby community. Seizing on the opportunity to earn some money and trusting the government when it announced that selling their blood was safe, her mother and father along with other relatives and friends traveled to the bleak no frills station to sell their blood. Unfortunately the blood was pooled and centrifuged to skim off the plasma and the red cells remaining were pooled and transfused back into the sellers permitting the spread of blood-borne diseases. Thus Maya's parents and many others, unwittingly became victims of Hepatitis and AIDS.

During the early years they had considered life in their village adequate. With little exposure to the bigger world outside they accepted the rhythm of their sparse existence, the monotonous days in the fields, the worry over the desperately needed harvest and the heartaches of losing a family member or close friend to death. They adhered to the teachings of Confucius and attempted to follow his words. "With yourself, live modestly, with work, do respectfully; with friends, abide loyalty," and as The Master had advised they spent much time and effort to "Make those close at home happy."

Loving parents and loving grandparents had raised Maya, Yugao and their older sister, Nashua. Uncles and aunts and other relatives lived nearby and the close knit extended family celebrated numerous festivals and enjoyed many family gatherings. When confronted with a drought, flood or an unusually meager harvest every member rushed to aid the relative or friend most in need. Maya and Yugao had gone to school and planned to continue their education but as time went on their sick parents and sick relatives meant that there was no one to work the land. Consequently, with no money for even the basic necessities higher education was a dream that vanished quickly.

As her parents' and other relatives' health continued to deteriorate a family council decided that Maya should go to Shanghai and find a job. Further, Yugao, in between his attempts to manage a small vegetable garden and a few pigs and chickens would travel to Shanghai once a month to get Maya's earnings and exchange it for folk medicine and other remedies to restore the health of those in need. Thus the future of the family was in the hands of Maya at eighteen years of age and Yugao, some three years younger.

Maya found Shanghai life exhilarating. She overlooked the gray-purple haze that blanketed the city as the factories and other endeavors spewed pollutants into the air. She was amazed at the grandeur of the hotels, the tall upscale apartment and office buildings and from a safe distance she watched the port's gigantic blue and white cranes move massive containers onto ocean-going ships destined for the United States and various European countries. She learned to weave safely through the pedestrian traffic between stops at the various hiring stations and she even hitched a ride or two on a new friend's scooter as they made their way to the Bund, also known as the People's Park, the city's largest.

When employed however, life took on a different flavor. There was little time to see the sights, little time to browse the shops and little time to engage in a lighthearted game of mahjong, the rules of which Maya had learned as a child at her grandmother's knee. Soon the young woman was counting the days until she could get away from the shirt factory and find a new job.

At the end of her year's contract Maya set out to make the rounds of the numerous hiring stations. A small stick thin man with bony hands and a somewhat unkempt white goatee hired Maya as part of a team preparing ladies elegant silk blouses and tailored suit dresses for shipment. Each garment was tagged with prepared labels indicating the price and size and then hung with care on special cloth covered hangers and encased in separate plastic bags. This meant that the merchandise had been prepared for sale at foreign mall stores and specialty shops by cheaper labor than labor at the destination point. Maya enjoyed her new work not far from where her scooter friend, Beibel, was employed but most of all she was delighted to find that her six day work week paid almost as much as her original seven day shirt factory job. She would have much to tell Yugao when he arrived at the end of the month.

On the morning of her first day off Maya and Beibel began a quick zigzag scooter ride through the downtown streets to one of the many outdoor markets tucked away on narrow streets. Soon the young women had joined the lookers and the shoppers moving in and out of the tiny stalls and the unique curiosity shops that were bulging with items that Maya and Beibel had only dreamt about. They lingered near the shelves of beautiful cloisonné pieces displayed near delicate porcelain and colorful glass figures and vases. They gingerly ran their fingers over the jade jewelry on display and exchanged childhood stories about being taught early on that jade had mystical powers to heal and restore the body and spirit. As Maya eyed the jade thumb ring she vowed that someday she'd have enough to buy jade for her parents and then they'd be well again, she was sure of it.

The two young women drifted through the main market where the luscious odor of jasmine hung in the air along with a blend of other delightful fragrances and spices they couldn't immediately identify. Tables were crammed with large bamboo cages for birds and smaller cages for crickets. Another merchant was proudly moving women's colorful silk garments shimmering in the warm breezes that were meant more for sale to tourists and the small emerging middle-class than the average factory worker. The scene was far removed from the general population that continued to suffer deprivation and severe hardships.

Eventually Maya and Beibel headed for the Yu Gardens where they lingered by a pond spanned by several small bridges and ate their spicy pork dumplings purchased from a nearby food vender. In between bites they shared their dreams for the future. Initially Maya considered her goals to be short and simple.

"I wish for good health for my family and to marry a rich man. That's all."

But when she hesitated for a moment and thought about it, she realized that that wasn't all. There were more hopes and dreams churning around in her head. She spoke of how she'd been tied to the land during her childhood and back then she'd been content to remain there forever and work the fields beside her family. But now all that had changed. After seeing bustling Shanghai she longed to live in one of the posh tall apartment buildings rising from the streets of the city. She turned and pointed up to the sky.

"I want to live way up there in the clouds and a rich man will make that happen."

Then with a hint of strong determination creeping into her voice Maya began the long sorrowful tale of her sister.

"Beibel I'll never, never do as my sister Nasha has done. No, I'm going to follow the government's policy and have only one baby."

Several years earlier during the first few years of Nasha's marriage to a distant cousin, Desheng, she discovered she was pregnant again after she had delivered a son the previous year. She ignored the dictates of her husband, who terrified of government reprisals for not following the country's One Child Policy insisted that she go to an abortion clinic. Nasha left her home early one dark and drizzly morning with little more than the clothes on her back, but instead of arriving at a government medical office she fled to relatives in an isolated part of the country. Out of sight of enforcement officials she delivered her second healthy baby boy. The unfortunate twist of the story is that the new baby by not being registered is destined to have a difficult life. More often than not an unregistered child is not accepted in school which means that his life choices are meager. Desheng still fearful of the government simply left one morning and never returned and Nasha was left with little means to support her two children.

Her sad plight touched Beibel and tugged once again at Maya's heartstrings and the two young women fell silent for several minutes lost deep in their own thoughts. Finally at Maya's urging Beibel spoke of her plans for the future.

"Well, first of all, I'm staying at my job for now and when I have enough money I'll give some to my family and then I'm heading to the university in Beijing."

It seemed as if the young woman had her life all planned out. She was full of chatter and more talkative than Maya had ever noticed before and when she recounted the highlights of her happy childhood a wide smile flashed across her face. She and her sister, Shuli, had been well educated by their

grandparents who had stressed education. Both had been university professors before the Cultural Revolution when they were fired for being "enemies
of the people." Beibel, full of confidence spoke of her dreams of becoming
an engineer.

"I'm good in math, my grandparents said so. Someday I'm going to help
build big projects all over the country, maybe something like the Three
Gorges Dam. And I'm going to travel. Oh, I want to see the tallest skyscraper
in the whole wide world. It's in Kuala Lumpur, Malaysia, you know. And you
know what else?" She didn't wait for an answer.

"I'm going to see the forty-foot Buddha in Sri Lanka. Can you believe it,
the statue was carved in the fifth century."

She looked directly at Maya and asked, "Did you ever want to go to Thai-
land? Well, I do. My grandfather says that they're building taller and taller
skyscrapers there. I don't care how long it takes I'm going to do it all."

She took a long deep breath while starring off in the distance. "My family
is going to be so proud of me just as proud of me as we all are of Shuli."

Beibel's face glowed with pride as she spoke of her sister who had studied
and trained in one of Beijing's largest hospitals and in less than a decade had
earned the reputation of being one of the capital city's most renowned sur-
geons. The conversation over, the two young women arm and arm strolled toward one of the parks ceremonial houses canopied by heavy leafy tree
branches and enjoyed the shade. Suddenly the idea of doing something won-
derfully impetuous hit Beibel.

"Let's get rid of these old faded jackets and pants and get dressed up and
go out to one of the bars."

When Maya hesitated about spending money Beibel soothed her con-
science.

"You know you really do deserve a treat, you've been working so hard."
Then she added with just a hint to impatience, "oh, come on, just this once."

They cut through the surging crowds of people and stopped at one of the
clothing shops on fashionable Nanjing Road. With reckless abandon each
purchased a sleek pair of black pants and similar colorful silk-blend yellow
blouses. Neither of them wanted to admit that with most of their money gone
they had little left for any other day-off activities for the remainder of the
month or longer.

As the night sky dropped across the city, Shanghai seemed to come alive
with thousands of glistening bright lights illuminating the river front prome-
nade, the high-rise hotels and the impressive entrances to bars and fine restaurants. Soon Maya and Beibel blended into the crowd guzzling beer, wine and
gin-tonic, tastes that were completely foreign to Maya and she found she enjoyed them all. As the night raced on the two young women danced and drank

and danced and drank and lost all track of time. They didn't want the evening to stop. They were seeing a part of life they'd only heard about. Perhaps it was the alcohol. Maybe it was the crowds hell bent on having a great time. Perhaps it was the months of living a cloistered life, but whatever it was, the evening would thrust Maya into a monumental state of sorrow and heartache that would cloud her life for endless days and nights ahead.

*　*　*

The first hint of dawn was still hours away when Yugao, in a deep and restful slumber felt gentle hands shaking him awake. His grandmother, fearful that he would miss his monthly ride to Shanghai fussed about him as he hurriedly downed his steaming tea and bowl of hot rice gruel and prepared to leave. The frail old lady with a wrinkled face and eyes full of sadness stood at the door and watched her grandson's lanky frame until it faded into the horizon. The young boy knew the monthly ritual by heart. Ride his bike along the bumpy back roads for several miles until he reached a main truck stopover where he'd catch up with his uncle Ge on his regular run to Shanghai. Ge, a small energetic man with cheerful dark eyes, a receding hair line and nicotine discolored fingers was one of the army of truckers rumbling along the highway in their eighteen wheelers brimming with computer chips, stereo speakers, plastic toys, shoes, kitchen hardware, statuary and vases or anything else that paid well. Arriving at the bustling container port the goods would then begin the next leg of the journey to various overseas ports of call.

Yugao and Ge never spoke much but understood each other completely. Since Yugao's and Maya's parents had fallen ill, Ge had taken Yugao under his wing and looked out for the boy. Any free time from the road was spent helping his young nephew work the vegetable garden and when needed, butchering a pig. More than once Ge had told Yugao that when his parents were well again in another year or two he'd find the youngster a job as a driver's helper. Secretly Ge carried little hope that their relatives and many of the villagers would ever recover. He heard and had listened well to the talk in the large cities of the curse of AIDS and Hepatitis that could be transmitted by unsafe blood handling and his thoughts shot back to the blood stations that had been so popular near their community several years earlier.

With his bike safely bound to the back of the truck, Yugao settled into his uncle's cab blackened by years of chain-smoking and watched Ge blend into the procession of noisy polluting road hogs moving eastward. Yugao was eyeing Ge's every movement through the coils of cigarette smoke, the racing of the engine and the shifting of the gears as they passed through drenching rains, strong gusts of wind and a fierce sun blazing in through the smoky windows. By mid afternoon they were streaming past fields of rippling green grains and busy carp farms and sadly they stopped to assist a fatal roll over of a truck only a few lengths ahead of them. Yugao was convinced his uncle was the best driver, the best anything.

Actually Ge had always been the pride and joy of the extended family. He was a human dynamo. He never ignored a perceived opportunity and was successful in whatever endeavor he had taken on. When he farmed his field was more productive than any of the other plots nearby. When his field caught the eye of a government official, rumor had it that Ge had been successful in bribing the official to allow him to bring his crops to market and keep much of the money he'd made hawking his grains, vegetables and chickens. When Ge heard of job openings on the road he joined the force and was in his fifth year of moving goods across the vast country. He was proud of his son who was attending law school in Canton and who would graduate within the year.

The late afternoon sun was beginning to face when Yugao awakened and glanced out the murky window. Ge was maneuvering the truck into the lengthy convoy of vehicles inching up to the container cranes on the south side of the port of Shanghai. At a selected spot Yugao retrieved his bike and with a final wave good-bye he set out to find Maya.

It had always worked before, why wasn't it working now? His sister would be waiting beside a subway stop and the quick exchange of money and news would begin. Yugao paced back and forth as a full moon appeared further illuminating the tall buildings and the crowds out for an evening of dining and dancing or just people watching. Realizing he couldn't wait any longer Yugao rode his bike back to his uncle's truck. As they headed westward Ge peppered Yugao with questions over and over and over. Was he sure, really sure he had stopped at the right place? Had Maya given any hint the preceding month that she wouldn't be at the selected spot? What could have happened to her? Could she be sick, or worse?

The city was so jam-packed and heavily policed by traffic cops that large trucks had few avenues in which to travel and Ge was uncomfortable letting the boy venture into unfamiliar parts. Sensing his nephew's anxiety Ge reassured Yugao that on his next visit he'd make arrangements to leave his truck for a few hours at the port and search for Maya himself. They couldn't have known that at that very moment Maya was struggling with her own day of hell.

*   *   *

It had never happened before, Maya sleeping through the dormitory's racket as the workers clopped around dressing and chattering before heading for their usual backbreaking day in the factories, mills or warehouses. It had been a wonderful night of dancing and meeting people but unfortunately Maya and Beibel had let the time slip away from them with the result that they had barely crawled into bed when it was almost time to get up. An hour or two later Maya awakened with a start and although woozy realized in a panic that she was late for work. As she dashed into the street she braced herself for her supervisor, Mr. Hu's wrath, whose favorite speech always seemed to be on the penalties of lateness. Indeed he always locked the doors after the workers were accounted for but this morning he left the main door slightly ajar.

Those who were acquainted with Mr. Hu would realize that it wasn't any act of kindness on his part but rather a ploy to catch the latecomer in a situation that only could be dealt with by docking her two days' pay. It was because of his harsh and unfair policies that Mr. Hu was quickly becoming rich on the backs of his workers. Any fines (and there were plenty of them for the slightest infractions) was pocketed by him and it was rumored that every time he increased the workers' quotas he received a special bonus from the shipping office that he no doubt used with relish to purchase numerous dietary delights that only added to his pudgy frame.

Mr. Hu, with a sinister smile that covered his moon-shaped face watched as Maya dashed from the bus towards the warehouse.

"You're late," he hissed.

Maya stood trembling before him.

"Perhaps I should dismiss you right now."

He cupped her chin and stuck his thick fingers into her cheeks while Maya lowered her eyes and studied the floor. She wanted to be anyplace but where she was but she needed this job desperately and in a coarse whisper she pleaded.

"Please, Mr. Hu, it won't happen again."

Mr. Hu savoring his hold over her slammed the door and snapped the lock before spitting out his instructions for the day.

"You're to have all the bolts of brocade on the fifth floor tagged, wrapped and ready for shipment by tomorrow morning."

Maya had hoped to slip out of the warehouse and dash to her meeting with Yugao but her heart fell when she realized that all the exits were completely locked and with the workers gone to other sections of the building for a few hours all the pounding she did on the doors was for naught. When she left work the next evening after an almost twenty-four hour shift with no food or rest she was exhausted but at least she was relieved that she'd completed her assignment and still had her job. Her days blended into weeks, whenever there was a rush job or an unusually difficult assignment it was Maya who Mr. Hu called on but she never complained not even when her pay was short and she lost her day off. She remembered her family and she counted and recounted her money hoping that at the end of the month she'd have enough to give Yugao to make up for the month they had missed each other.

Uncle Ge hadn't been able to return to Shanghai and search for Maya. One week his run brought him back and forth to the bustling Pearl River delta port at Shenzhen, other assignments included crossing into Hong Kong and then northward to truck tractors, plastics and textiles into the busy docks at Qingdao. He even was gone on the road when Maya and Yugao's parents gave up their fight to live.

Yugao and his grandmother watched helplessly as the two began to fail rapidly. Yugao's father, who had been jaundiced for some time, eventually became too weak to even cough. The whites of his eyes turned a deep yellow, his abdomen, legs and feet were swollen. He was wracked with delirium and pain and as the days went on he became less responsive to any stimulus. He died one morning, as the sun was just about ready to creep across the village fields. Within a few hours a district health worker arrived to register the deceased father. After the necessary paper work she diagnosed Yugao's mother in the last stages of tuberculosis, no doubt the result of the AIDS virus she had contracted from unsafe blood. The sick woman found it harder and harder to breathe and finally slipped away late in the evening two short days after her husband.

As the family prepared for the funerals they thought of Maya. They mourned, tramped to a temple and thought of Maya. They burned red paper in honor of the dead and brought the ash from the paper home and thought of Maya and slowly, ever so slowly the resentment began to build. It was her fault that her ailing parents hadn't received all the medicine they needed — especially the folk medicine that according to family lore had been successful in treating a plethora of ailments during the centuries. The special herbs and roots and animal parts had always worked well for them and they would have worked now had Maya not relinquished her duty and met Yugao when she should have.

Finally Maya was permitted a day off but certainly not due to Mr. Hu's generosity. For several days he'd noticed that she had all the symptoms of over work, the listless walk, the frayed nerves, the eyes tired and sad. Pondering the situation he decided that it might be better to give her time off and salvage one of his best workers than to continually have her labor fourteen and sixteen hour days non-stop and become too ill to work. While the busy streets of Shanghai called to Maya she decided to head for home. It still bothered her that it had been weeks since she'd exchanged money and news with Yugao. With a hug she bid Beibel good-bye and worked her way to the docks where it wasn't hard to catch a ride westward. All the truckers needed to hear was that she was Ge's niece and she was welcomed aboard. It was well after midnight when the truck rolled into a sleepover station. Maya disappeared down an old rutted red clay back road and headed for home. It was almost dawn when she came across a farmer and his mules clopping along and for the rest of the journey she endured the old man's aimless gossip and his uncomfortable wagon.

There was no grand homecoming with hugs and smiles through the tears. Her grandmother and brother sipped hot tea and avoided her eyes entirely. Even as they ignored her questions their resentment smoldered. When Yugao did speak his voice was full of resentment and anger and the rest of the day went from bad to worse. Relatives came by. Some brushed past her without any comment. Others, especially the children stared at her with hostile eyes. Several days later the situation hadn't improved nor would it ever improve if something drastic hadn't occurred.

* * *

Beibel sensing that something was very wrong when Maya hadn't returned to the city and her job left Shanghai to find Maya. There she set eyes on a person she hardly recognized. Maya, refusing to eat for several days had lost weight, her eyes were red from frequent crying and the toll of her being ostracized was evident. No matter what Beibel attempted she couldn't bring Maya out of her depression and more than once she winced as she heard Maya sob, "I've disgraced my ancestors."

Beibel left with an idea running around in her head. Within days she had arrived in Beijing to meet her sister, Shuli who heard every detail of Maya's agony more times than she could count. At Beibel's insistence Shuli took a few days off and by the time they arrived in Maya's village, Shuli was read to go into high gear.

She organized the children and sent them out to gather their parents, relatives and friends and as the evening sun began to fade a crowd assembled somewhat reluctantly in an old dilapidated barn to see the "top doctor from Beijing." Shuli pulled no punches, in between the meandering children and animals she presented the facts of the unsafe blood work of years ago and its harsh consequences throughout the country. Further she gently discounted the importance of the folk medicine in this instance that everyone had put so much faith in to restore health. She continued talking and explained the harsh working conditions in the nation's factories and warehouses, the lock ups, the unhealthy stuffy workrooms, the unattainable quotas and the constant scrutiny. Lastly she spoke of Maya and her devotion to her family, laboring day after day and willing to give "the fruits of her labor to her family."

Was it Shuli's neatly pressed white coat, her forceful voice and her professional demeanor that held their attention? Was it the sight of the young woman slumped into an old rickety metal chair with tears running down her face that reached their hearts? More than likely it was a combination of both. Before Shuli and Beibel left, the doctor ministered to the settlement's people accompanied by Maya and slowly, ever so slowly the people's cold attitude towards Maya began to thaw.

That was nearly a year ago. Maya has remained in her village sandwiched in between the generations. She takes care of her grandmother who is increasingly becoming more feeble and at times is crotchety and domineering. Sadly her sister Nasha is ill most of the time with a medical problem not yet diagnosed. Maya looks after Nasha's boys and sees to it they have schooling and enough to eat. She is often sighted bent over in the vegetable garden beside Yugao and it is Maya who prepares the crops for the market, which is the sole source of their income. Thus her days are full and demanding but she hasn't lost sight of her dream to return to Shanghai someday and "marry a rich man." While someday in the future that may be possible for now she is content to follow Confucius' admonition, "Comfort the elderly, confide in friends, caress the young."

She receives envelopes of literature on a somewhat regular basis from Shuli. Maya calls the villagers together and they read and discuss hygiene, the importance of an adequate diet and the signs of health problems that need attention. Beibel has entered Beijing University and is busy taking the required classes before being admitted to the Engineering School. While miles separate these three women they remain close in their hearts and minds as part of global sisterhood striving to make life better for themselves and their countrymen.

Chapter Thirteen

"Courage is doing what you're afraid to do. There can be no courage unless you're scared."

—Eddie Rickenbacker

Margie barely stirred when the alarm shattered the bedroom's silence. Could it be time to get up already? She laid there in the semi-darkness for a moment enjoying the quiet and mentally planning her busy day. Today was going to be special, very special. After eighteen years as a clerk she was finally getting her well-deserved promotion to Manager. She couldn't count how many times she'd been passed over and a man had been rewarded with the coveted position.

She'd always considered herself a patient person and rationalized that perhaps the time wasn't right but eventually even she became weary of waiting. There was no way she could rationalize it any longer, in plain English she was trapped in a dead-end job in the personnel department. Following a heated exchange with the departing Human Resource Manager about discrimination against women, her remarks had gone to the top. She could only guess what went on in Mr. Hahn's office but whatever it was, it must have gone in her favor and she considered that she'd won. She didn't often see the president even though he'd been at his post for decades. Rumor had it that he ran the company with an iron fist and no one ever dared challenge him well, that is until Margie came along. She concentrated on her promotion and all the perks that went with it not the least of which was more money, more money to cope with the family's mounting medical bills.

Tom, her devoted husband of twenty years was failing. Countless years of heavy smoking had left its ugly mark on his lungs. Summers were the worst an unusually hot and sunny day meant dangerous ozone levels. Margie and Tom knew the radio warnings by heart.

"This is a Code Red day for Philadelphia and vicinity with heat indexes in the triple digits." Oh, how she hated to hear that last warning "unhealthy for sensitive groups."

Margie was slipping into one of her best dresses, (she wanted to look her best today), when she noticed the scent of freshly brewed coffee wafting into the bedroom. Dear Tom, he still insisted on brewing the coffee even though his persistent coughing left him weak and in severe pain for most of the morning. Margie tried not to be obvious as she and Tom stood facing each other losing themselves in idle conversation but her heart sank. He looked unusually pale this morning, there wouldn't be any brief strolls in the nearby park today. Dear Tom, he had always been there for her and their daughter Lisa. Now they both needed her.

"This Saturday I'm going with Lisa and no one will stop us." Margie was bent on a mission. She was livid the previous week when Lisa had returned home in a state of panic after being harassed outside an abortion clinic and bumped around enough that she didn't make it inside. Margie passed the clinic every morning as the bus sped downtown. It seemed as if the scene never changed, no matter the weather, no matter the seasons. A few gray-haired women alongside men, some young some old, who'd never have to make a similar decision about their own bodies were steadfastly praying and hoisting signs several feet away from the clinic's entrance, "Don't Murder Your Baby." An abortion was the only way out for Lisa. The three of them knew that. There was little room in the cramped two-bedroom apartment and little money for a new addition to the family. Most of Margie's money was going for Tom's prescriptions and office visits that were occurring more frequently. They had talked well past midnight many nights during the past three weeks when Lisa's boyfriend of two years left for the Army after declaring that he wanted neither marriage nor a baby.

Through the years Margie had been tirelessly dedicated to the issues of Pro-Choice and enthusiastically had marched in several demonstrations, rain or shine. As Lisa grew older she always tagged along with her mother. There always seemed to be a rally or march to attend and it wasn't long before the struggle for women's rights became paramount in both their lives. Margie could never have guessed that one day her own daughter would be a candidate for an abortion. Always fearful of a crisis Margie had been saving steadily through the years for some unknown emergency. Now she knew that this was that emergency. But it would all be over on Saturday, Lisa could go on with her life and build a career with endless possibilities. Margie never ceased to marvel at the vast opportunities for today's young women, certainly more than the meager prospects her generation faced. When she started working a career meant spending a few years as a teacher, a nurse, a typist or the ever-popular stenographer or secretary before marriage.

Margie boarded the same bus, reached the same seat, nodded to the same familiar faces with the same smiles or scowls as she had done for endless weeks, months and years. She looked out the window and yet was seeing nothing, she was sliding into a bottomless pit of worry. What if she became sick or disabled and was unable to work? What about Tom's condition, she knew he wasn't getting any better but what if he got worse? How could she ever go on without the love of her life? And what if Lisa made another mistake? Margie felt she was being weighed down, so much was on her shoulders. She thought of her mother, Helen who had never worked outside the home. She'd gone from her parents home to her own home and been content to be a housewife. Unfortunately with little health benefits for the miners she was left with little more than a crude shack and a mountain of bills when her husband's life was snuffed out in a tragic mining accident in the Pennsylvania coal country. Margie lugging suitcases crammed with food and clothing visited her mother regularly and she always left with a heavy heart. Soon poor medical care and pneumonia took its toll and after they laid Helen to rest in a small, rocky cemetery beside her husband, Margie never went back.

The bus lurched to a sudden stop at the downtown terminal and Margie melted into the crowd busily heading for their offices in the heart of Philadelphia's financial district. The walk always invigorated her and she felt her grit and determination returning. Today would be a special day—nothing would spoil it. It had to be—the fate of her family rested on her.

A few minutes later Margie pushed open the elegant brass and glass doors and made her way to her new office. Easing into the brown leather chair that had seen better days, she glanced around the room drinking in its smallness. Oh, well it was a start anyway, she reasoned. If she'd thought about it she would have realized that making coffee was no longer her chore but old habits die-hard. She made her way to the small alcove serving as a kitchen as she had done countless Mondays before the weekly department meetings. At first she paid little attention to the murmuring in the corridor a few feet away but then her heart almost skipped a beat. A group of department managers, some old enough to be her father were commiserating on the office news.

"Well, it looks as if we're gonna have to put up with the bitch Margie as a manager now."

"Yeah, I hear she raised enough hell that they had to . . . yeah had to give the old gal the job."

"Well, you gotta admit she's always been on the ball. I know she'd helped me out of a jam more than once."

"Hey, Bob. You ain't gone soft on us are you? What the hell are you doin' sticking up for a woman?"

Margie listened to an embarrassed mumble. "Naw, but she's been here a long time, you gotta admit that."

"Well, I don't give a damn how long she's been here, the job should've gone to a man. Look at us, we're all men." She winced at the laughter.

"How the hell are we gonna chew the fat with a woman? No sense asking her to join us for a drink after work on Fridays, goddamn women. They're always pushing . . . always pushing. Always wanting to change things." A chorus of "yeah's" followed.

Margie stood perfectly still almost trying not to breathe lest she be heard. The half-full coffee filter was shaking in her hands and some of the coffee grounds spilled over the small counter and onto the floor. By the time she entered the boardroom (without the coffee) she had regained her composure and with detached calmness she accepted the half-hearted applause on her promotion with a stiff smile. She put names to the voices she'd overheard and realized that the situation was even worse than she'd thought. She was mired in a sea of chauvinism that was pervasive throughout the company and she wondered how many times she'd have to prove herself or if she'd even last through it all.

Margie found it hard to concentrate as her special day moved on. The females she had worked with drifted in and out, giving her hugs, congratulations and some lingered to chat a bit. Fortunately they had the good sense not to notice her cubbyhole with not even a bookcase to warm it. The good sense not to notice her old scratched desk with wobbly legs and the good sense not to mention that her door was still without her name. Finally it was quitting time and when everyone left for the day she had the chance to stroll past the other manager's spacious offices and to compare them to hers. What she saw only added to her resentment. There were fancy over-sized mahogany desks sitting aside tall bookcases bulging with cascading plants, family photos, books, trophies and other special mementos. What a contrast! She compared her almost threadbare carpet to the thick oriental rugs in the other offices and gave a long sigh. She was being treated as a second-class citizen just because of her gender and it hurt, it hurt deeply.

Despite the energy of the crowd heading for home Margie couldn't shake her frustration and disappointment. She knew she'd have to perk up because she didn't want share her feelings with Tom and Lisa and have them upset. She decided she'd put on a happy face and tell them that her day had been great.

"You'll have to come in to see my new office someday." But deep in her heart she hoped that they would never take her up on that.

The week wore on and early Saturday morning Lisa and her mother trying desperately to ignore the sarcastic chants of an anti-abortion group entered the clinic. When mother and daughter returned home a few hours later Tom held both of them close.

The cruel hot summer that at times seemed endless finally gave way to the refreshing coolness of autumn. Trees swaying in the breeze were beginning to shed their gold and scarlet leaves and the whole city seemed to be bathed in a beautiful splash of colors. This had always been Margie's favorite time of the year but she had too much on her mind this year to give much notice to the change of seasons. It wasn't long before the days were becoming noticeably shorter and cooler with a hint of frost in the air some mornings and now everyone's thoughts were turning to the magic of winter. Margie was still getting the cold shoulder from most of her male coworkers but through much practice she was becoming more adept at ignoring it. However nothing could have prepared her for her experience as she answered Mr. Hahn's summons.

He motioned to her to sit in a large comfortable chair in front of his desk. At first he seemed pleasant enough as they continued their idle chitchat about the traffic and weather. But when he started his spiel she decided she hated him. He announced his plan. She was to get an assistant.

"He'll take some of the burden off of you. An . . . I'm happy to tell you that the management's decided to transfer a fine young man from Accounting. He'll take your place should you ever decide to leave."

He cleared his throat and continued to drone on.

"Actually, you should be quite proud of this unique arrangement. Your department is being reorganized and the other department heads don't have an special assistant that would take over as much responsibility as he will with you."

Margie felt the color drain from her face. She knew what had happened. Her job had been watered down to make way for another male who needed "to get his career on the fast track." The last remark was particularly scathing.

"He has a wife and child to support so I know you can appreciate his position."

It was only days later that she learned that the "fine young man" was a son of one of the president's closest golfing buddies. Before the week had ended Margie had her new assistant Karl and their awkward relationship began. Who would do what? Who would be responsible for the hiring, the initiation of permanent employees into the company's pension fund, performance reviews, disciplinary actions, the firings and other items specific to the Human Resource Department?

At first she had to admit that he really was a likable fellow but as time went on she discovered that more and more of her responsibilities were eroding and ending up on Karl's shoulders. Some days she had little to do and it graded on her that she had to carry mountains of files back and forth to an assistant in a large comfortable office far superior to her own lean diggings. More and more she was beginning to feel trapped. She couldn't forget that she was her family's sole breadwinner and she couldn't give the company chauvinists any reason to fire her. Still more than once she asked herself how much longer she would be able to put up with the situation.

Perhaps she reached the end of her endurance one morning after spending most of the night tending to Tom and trying to soothe his pain and constant coughing. Dozing off just before dawn, she was startled by the alarm and slowly dragged herself out of bed. When she arrived at the bus stop her heart skipped a beat. All she could see of the bus was it's smoky pollution as it sped down the street. A later bus got her to work but the whole morning had been a series of frustrations. Tired and discouraged she sat at her wobbly desk and decided that she had no choice. If she ever wanted things to change she'd have to take a bold step. A plan had been lounging in the back of her mind and she decided to act on it!

Her first step was the library after work where she spent many evenings and weekends reading everything she could find on sexual discrimination in the workplace. She wanted to be well versed on the subject and after she had compiled enough detailed information she contacted the Equal Employment Opportunity Commission. By the third meeting with an EEOC representative, Margie had memorized portions of the Civil Rights Act of 1964 which prohibits employment discrimination based on race, color, religion, sex, or natural origin.

She had a case the representative agreed. But did she really want to put in the countless hours that a complaint would require? Further, was she prepared to cope with all the consequences after the complaint was filed? Margie didn't hesitate. After spending numerous sleepless nights mulling over the situation she was positive she'd made the right decision. For her the issue was too important to let die.

She had a lot to think about and more often than not she remained in her stuffy little office during lunch hour, pouring over the inch thick mass of EEOC correspondence and evaluating additional information from the Fair Employment Practices Agency. The offices usually were pretty much deserted at that time except for the receptionists. Perhaps that was why Margie was so startled by a faint knock on the door. She went into a full panic mode, she wanted to grab the papers and stash them in her desk but she didn't have time. The second knock had an urgency about it.

Margie couldn't remember ever seeing her up close before. She had the look of money and class with her designer black dress and bold gold jewelry.

Her glossy auburn hair framed a pleasant face with a faint touch of make-up and her well-manicured hands held a Gucci handbag.

"Margie, may I call you Margie?" She didn't wait for an answer and continued. " I have been hearing some pretty remarkable things about you over dinner. I am Betty Hahn. Bill Hahn's wife."

There was no place to sit so they stood staring at each other. Margie would have liked to cover the papers across her desk but it was too late. Betty Hahn already had picked up a few pages that had caught her eye with bold EEOC across the letterhead. Margie's heart sank but as it turned out it didn't need to. What Betty Hahn told her was a real shocker.

She was disgusted by her husband's order to Karl to present himself once a week for dinner and sick of listening to all the plotting and their boring macho jokes about the company's female employees. She was appalled by her husband's machinations. She knew that Karl wasn't there because Bill was impressed by him or even liked him although her husband talked a different story. She didn't leave out any of the unpleasant details. Indeed she remembered what went on word by word.

"Son, you're doing fine, I've got faith in you, the company's got faith in you. Keep up the good work. We have big plans for you, Karl—big plans."

Betty was talking non-stop now as she continued. Margie was hearing things she never thought she'd hear. It was the same every week. After dinner Karl and Bill would move to the den, find their favorite oversized easy chairs and relax while sipping their brandy and puffing away on their expensive cigars. Betty would excuse herself and linger in another room but she kept an ear open to the conversation. As usual Bill's voice was loud and clear.

"You know, son, department heads in this organization have always been males and I damn well want to keep it like that." Then he'd bellow, "find me a loop-hole son. We don't want this 'women's lib gal' to start a trend. Find me a way to get rid of her. You got that?"

What is it about the best-laid plans of mice and men? Well, apparently Bill's best-laid plans were not paying off. As time went on Karl was becoming more and more frustrated and Bill didn't like what he was hearing. More than once, actually more times that Betty wanted to hear, after their weekly dinners Karl's report would take Bill step by step through the daily workings of the Human Resource department. Margie was efficient, he couldn't deny that, when he asked her to work on specific projects, not only did she do it proficiently but more often than not, to his chagrin, they were completed ahead of schedule.

While Bill was still satisfied with his maneuverings and still confident a solution would be found to the problem of female managers, something was happening to Karl. Over the past few weeks he had given the situation a lot of thought and came to the conclusion that he was fed-up with Bill. Not one to keep his feelings hidden for long he began to show signs of boredom listening to Bill's non-stop blabbing about his favorite company practices that "kept women in their place." Always a good judge of people it wasn't long before Bill noticed Karl's fidgeting and lack of interest.

"Let's hear it Karl, what's eating you?"

Karl took a gulp of his brandy, swallowed hard and began. He was becoming weary of the subterfuge. He wanted a "real position to get his career back on track." He reminded Bill that he'd majored in Marketing and graduated top of his class at the University of Pennsylvania and probably thinking he had nothing more to lose, he stood up and blurted out.

"Goddamn it, Bill, I'm sick of plain old personnel work."

"Now hold on Karl. We can work something out."

Both men were deep in thought and Betty smiled as she remembered waiting for the fireworks to start but the room remained strangely quiet. Betty laughed and looked at Margie.

"You know I think you could've heard a pin drop in that room that night."

She mentioned how surprised she was that Bill had said nothing and just sat there chomping on his cigar. Then at his insistence more brandy was poured and she heard the sound of the glasses touching. The two men became louder and more obnoxious. Betty described how she sat in the next room thumbing through a fashion magazine and finally when she could stand it no longer she stormed in.

"You are both chauvinist asses." She continued in spite of their startled look. "To put a good employee through this just because the employee's a woman is ludicrous. And what will you two good old boys do when your daughters come home someday frustrated and disgusted because they're facing the same situation? Well, tell me. What will you two do? "Huh? Well, go ahead tell me."

Of course there was more, Karl, sensing a family catastrophe on the horizon, found the door. The Hahn's bickering continued well past dawn when Bill stormed out of the house and headed for the office. Each of them was carrying their own banners, each of them was convinced they were right and no one was prepared to give an inch.

Betty's voice dropped as she added, "we haven't spoken since that night." Margie was still in a daze and when Betty asked for more EEOC sheets she barely nodded.

"Well, I don't know what I've accomplished, he's so stubborn. But I think I made him think about his own daughters."

She held up the pages and triumphantly added, "This is precisely what I need. He doesn't need legal difficulties and he detests lawsuits."

Before Margie could reply Betty had folded the papers into her handbag and stared at the floor.

"It's too late for me, Margie. I partied through four years at a prestige college and along the way I discovered how to impress the so-called in crowd. I learned well how to entertain properly and to make appropriate small talk at boring cocktail parties with the best of them." She continued, her voice dripping in sarcasm.

"I learned to pick the best fabrics, the best decorator and the best clothes. Bill had big plans, such big plans and I became part of them. After all, I was the proper wife, that all-important asset so his career would flourish and he'd reach the top."

Margie noticed a far away look in her eyes and there was an embarrassed pause before she continued.

"Oh, sure, along the way I tried to develop my own thoughts and opinions but, as you can expect, anything I said was met with lack of interest, sometimes even ridicule or worse. You want to know why I put up with it?" She didn't wait for Margie to answer. "Well, I put up with all of it because I didn't want to give up the chic houses, the Mercedes, the elegant parties, and of course the great shopping trips to Milan and Rome. And yes, I really looked forward to the wonderful vacations without Bill to the Greek Islands. But you know what happened along the way? I remained the dutiful little wife on the outside but I never gave up my ideas for our daughters. Many evenings when we were alone I talked to them about being their own persons, having their own opinions and goals. My dream for them is that they have interesting lives, interesting and fulfilling careers and not to ever be saddled with limited choices just because they are females." There was a meaningful pause and she looked intently at Margie.

"By the way, no one needs to know we had this conversation."

She turned, reached for the door and was gone, the only thing left was the fragrance of her expensive perfume. Margie sat down on the edge of her desk her nerves taut. The president's wife had let her in on her very private moments and she didn't know whether to feel uplifted or terrified. What would the outcome of all of this be?

It would be great to say that everything took a fast about-face after Betty's visit but of course it didn't. Things moved along slowly, the very projects that Margie had previously lost came back at a snail's pace but they did come back. Karl had fallen from favor and rumor had it he was leaving the company but not before informing Margie that she would be moved to a new office after the first of the year. The whole incident didn't leave Margie unscathed. At times she felt as if she was still under siege. While she felt she had won a small victory, she kept her EEOC project safely on the back burner lest the gains she'd made would suddenly unravel.

When recruiting new talent at local collages and universities, she always managed to encourage resumes from female aspirants. Realizing that they would have to be twice as good, she was unbending in selecting only the best and the brightest young women. She lost some battles of course but she also won some and as time went on she felt she was winning more than she was losing at the weekly staff meetings. She learned to live with the aloofness of the old department heads and reviled in her new spacious office with a long window affording her a spectacular view of the city's impressive skyline. She couldn't help but chuckle that her office was right smack in the middle of the same men she had overheard near the coffee room on her first day as a Manager. She heard through the grapevine that Mr. Hahn had called a special meeting one night after the office had emptied. Apparently he had spoken to the male attendees at great length about the problems EEOC could give them and they received a carefully tailored message loud and clear that no one at the top wanted any lawsuits and the unpleasant publicity that it could create.

The days became calmer and if Tom had noticed that she'd been unusually tense and preoccupied during the previous months, he never mentioned it. He was completely house bound and health bound now, never far from his oxygen, but she still had him. They would spend hours talking about happier times when both of them were working and casting an optimistic eye to the future. Lisa was in her second year at the university and doing well. She'd put the past behind her and they never mentioned the abortion or the sense of relief it provided them.

Philadelphia's hot steamy summer had arrived and Margie remembered that it was almost a year to the day when she'd upset the status quo. Mr. Hahn was still at the company's helm and if they passed each other in the hall there were no niceties, no small talk, some days not even any recognition. Only once during an award meeting did he even acknowledge that she was there and handed her a plaque with the inscription "Most Proficient Department."

Margie took pride in the fact that several young women had been hired and were starting their climb up the corporate ladder and building careers in Accounting, Acquisitions and in Human Relations. They were exceptional young women full of promise and equipped for success in the corporate world. More than once they gravitated to Margie's desk after the other offices had emptied. She enjoyed her roll as mentor but no longer bored them with the drawn out details of her struggle to get to the top. She surmised that they wouldn't have understood her patience, there were of a different generation.

The following year was not a good one. Tom had been hospitalized more than once and by year's end his heart had given out. On a cloudy cold day she and Lisa watched sadly as his coffin was slowly lowered into the ground. A week or two later Lisa left to attend graduate school in Boston and Margie felt more alone that she'd ever been. After a few restless weeks at home following the funeral and trying to cope with her grief she returned to work and was grateful for the diversion. She hated to go home to the empty apartment but was dealing with her loss the best she could. During one of the many evenings she stayed well past quitting time, Mr. and Mrs. Hahn walked by. Assuming that the two women had never met, Bill Hahn introduced his wife to Margie. Neither Betty nor Margie made any mark of recognition but for a fleeting second their eyes met and they knew that they had connected.

They are two women whose paths had crossed somewhat precariously, each with entirely different lifestyles, with entirely different problems and yet they found the courage to unite to make a change, albeit small, either for themselves or for their daughters. Social standing couldn't separate them entirely for they are alike in their thinking that all women must have equitable access to opportunities in the work place. When the skills and talents females have developed or are in the process of developing are utilized in the marketplace, factories or in the corporate world then the world truly becomes a better place.

Chapter Fourteen

"We must be willing to get rid of the life we've planned, so as to have the life that is waiting for us."

—James Campbell

The small dark blue sedan made the last turn on the ribbon of road winding around Aguadilla's most prestigious hotel and came to a stop in the employees' parking lot. A pleasant looking (but a slightly overweight) woman emerged and headed for the back door as she had done so many mornings before. Gena moved through the massive laundry room with its row of oversized washers and dryers filled to capacity, some with linens and others tumbling the large fluffy pale blue-green towels boldly emblazed with the hotel's insignia. Good, she thought as she checked the laundry crew's time sheets. Everyone had signed in and the machines were humming through their cycles. And as she had done every morning for the last seventeen years she poked her head into the kitchen to greet the head chef directing his helpers who were busily engaged in filling special orders for breakfast. At another station a pastry chef was engrossed in producing an elaborately decorated wedding cake, no doubt the first of many he would be called on to create during the tourist season which was upon them. One could always know what time of year it was in Puerto Rico by the visitors to the island. From December to April all the hotels were busy and many constantly filled to capacity.

Gena continued to her small alcove of an office marked 'Housekeeper' on the main floor, a few feet behind a massive mirror at the check-in desk of one of the city's most prestigious hotels. She sat at her desk and thumbed through the large wall calendar before catching one of the brass and glass elevators to the top floor to check on the maids who were on duty. Some of the girls still in secondary school needed a close eye not unlike how she was when she started work. She thought back to her first day when she constantly had to fight back the tears. Victor, her husband of barely a year and a half had left for New York City. At the suggestion of one of his professors, a few months after receiving his master's degree in finance, Victor had announced to Gena's shock and dismay that he was leaving shortly for New York, alone.

"It's the place to be after all. That's where the opportunities are and I'm going for it." But that wasn't the way it was supposed to be.

For all of her teen years Gena and Victor had dated. He had been her first and only love and from the night of her quinceañera they had been inseparable. The evening had come together like one grand fairy tale. In a pale pink full-skirted taffeta ball gown that her mother had spent weeks sewing, Gena had arrived at the parish church on the arm of her proud father. After the small religious ceremony, family and friends had moved to one of the city's more elaborate hotels for an evening of celebration. The ancient custom was still a hard and fast one for her family. Even though funds were not plentiful through the years they always seemed to have enough that every young female relative was feted at a ceremony designed to announce that the young girl had become a woman. Superstition had it that the first non-family male the girl danced with would become her husband so it was no surprise a few years later to notice Gena sporting a tiny diamond and giving glowing reports of her future with Victor. They planned their wedding to coincide with her graduation from secondary school after which they'd pack up and leave for New York and take advantage of every opportunity there and life would be great! However a few short weeks before their first wedding anniversary, Gena delivered a baby girl, with a fuzz of ebony hair and deep brown eyes who they named Reva and within a short time it became evident that their well thought out plans were rapidly unraveling.

"You'll have to stay here with the baby until I get settled in New York. Don't worry, I'll send you some money."

For the first few years the checks were ample and frequent. Gena lived for Victor visits; a week or two during the summer and a few days at Christmas even though at times her husband appeared withdrawn and secretive. As time went on more often than not the visits ended on a stressful note.

"Vic, why can't Reva and I move to New York with you?"

"I'm just not set up yet for a family. It's a dog-eat-dog world there and I have to spend a lot of late nights at the office."

"Well, just when are you going to be set-up?"

Gena hated it when she sank into sarcasm but she was disgusted with her role of being a part-time wife and when she waved good-by to her husband at the airport she could feel her resentment mounting. However, as usually happened by the time she arrived back home she'd decided to make the best of the situation. She had always considered herself a patient person and determined to get through it by holding fast onto Victor's last words, "the good life is just around the corner." Several months later as she was still waiting for the "good life" the checks began to arrive smaller and less frequent and she listened to Vic complain that his job was "not panning out." After months of worrying and scrimping to get by Gena left little Reva with her mother and became a maid at the hotel. Thus began her career not in New York as a wife and mother, but a maid in Aguadilla's main hotel. Three years later she stood nervously in the hotel manager's office, received accolades for her work and was promptly promoted to Housekeeper. To her dismay her pride in her new position only seemed to hand Victor another reason to maintain their long-distance marriage.

"Wow, that's great. Well, you can't leave there now, a good promotion like that doesn't open up everyday." After he added, "stick with it for the time-being," she heard the click of the phone and it went dead.

Time moved along, Reva entered school and Gena's days became routine. Work, home, work, home. Watch for the mail. Listen for the phone. For months she was without a telephone number as Victor moved to "a better apartment, something with a little more breathing room."

It appeared as just a regular day not unlike any other. At times, to Gena's annoyance the young maids seemed more interested in the hotel's gossip than noting the guests' special requests for a softer pillow, additional towels, or an extra blanket. She had frequently entered the maid's supply room to find the young women giggling and sharing a secret about someone's love life but today after her routine checking, floor by floor, everything appeared to be in order. As she stormed across the lobby she was still rehashing Victor's latest note.

"Things up here are still up in the air and I'm looking around for another position. I have a few great leads for an international bank on the West Side. I'll let you know."

She felt like tearing the paper into shreds but instead rolled it into a tight ball and tossed it into the trash. She couldn't have known that she was about to be tossed about with a bolt out of the blue, but then most tragedies come without any warning. The desk clerk with a somber look spreading across her face motioned to Gena.

"Gena, it's your father. He's . . . well, he's at the hospital, something about a heart attack. Your mother just called."

The hospital's corridor seemed to go on forever. When she finally found her mother it was as if the woman had aged twenty years in one afternoon. While mother and daughter sat together holding each other and watching the old man sink lower and lower, doctors and nurses with stern faces entered, checked the machines and left saying little. A few days later before the first hint of morning the machines were turned off, and Gena and her mother and a few relatives who had continued their vigil were left to deal with their thoughts and their loss. Gena would recall later that the next few days were one big blur. Victor came home for the funeral and remained silent and respectful as he served as one of the pallbearers. Before he and Gena had time to talk he left as suddenly as he had arrived. For Gena the shock and the sorrow of loosing her father was hard enough to deal with but it was only part of the trials that were about to unfold around her.

It happened slowly and without spotting at first. Gena stopping by her mother's house before dropping Reva off at school and heading for work, always speaking to her mother and getting no reply. A few weeks later it hit Gena. No matter when she entered the house her mother was lying in bed in a stuffy room, with windows tightly shut and blinds drawn, either staring at the ceiling or pretending to sleep. Attempts to talk to the woman were ignored until late one evening she answered Gena's attempts to get her to move with, "Leave me along. I have nothing to live for with your father gone."

Relatives helped move Gena and Reva out of their house and into her mother's home. It took some doing to rearrange furniture, sort and send some things to storage but soon life took on its own routine. Doctor's visits became the norm and struggles with the despondent woman were frequent. When Victor called he appeared to be relieved.

"You can't leave your mother now, you know that. We'll just have to put off our plans to be together for the time being."

She hated to admit he was right but deep down she knew he was.

Some days nothing seems to go right and today was one of those days. Gena had tossed and turned all night. She'd awakened several times to the sound of her mother sobbing and rushed to comfort her. When she slipped back into her own bed Gena tossed and turned for the remainder of the night. By dawn her nerves were on edge and she had to make every effort to drag herself out of bed and leave for work. By the time she pulled into the parking lot she felt as if she was at the breaking point. At her desk even the hotel's strong coffee didn't seem to help. The previous evening had been a nightmare. When Gena arrived home from work, Reva, with disheveled hair and clothes awry was sitting on the sofa with a young man named Max. After he quickly escaped into the night mother and daughter exchanged many harsh words.

"You know the rules. You're not to have any boys in the house when I'm not here. You know your grandmother is not well."

"Max just isn't 'any' boy Mom. We're in love and pledged to each other. And I'm going to see him no matter what you say. And anyway we are going to get married some day and have a real marriage, not like what you have."

They sparred tensely for over an hour with Gena attempting to give Reva advice all the while endeavoring to face down her daughter's rebellion. By the time Gena finally rushed into the bedroom to check on her mother she had completely lost her patience and her composure.

"Mama, you've got to stop this. You've got to pull yourself together, I know you miss Papa, I miss him too but it's so hard for me to just stand by and watch you hurting so much."

At first it appeared that her mother was tuning her out which only added to Gena's frustration. When the old woman sat up in bed Gena reached out and grabbed her unsympathetically by the shoulders and began screaming her litany of complaints.

"You're getting weaker and weaker every day. No matter what I've tried to do to help you nothing works. You won't take my advice. You won't take the doctor's advice. You won't swallow your medicine and you refuse to say anything to the counselors we visit. You're going to kill yourself lying here, refusing to eat. For god's sake tell me. Tell me. How can I help you?"

Gena didn't realize that the more she talked and screeched the harder she held onto her mother's shoulders. When reality set in she was so ashamed she dashed from the room. A short time later she found herself racing along the beach not far from the house and soon she had blended into a small crowd assessing the furry of a late spring tropical storm as it blew along the island's north west coast apparently gaining strength as it headed further west to Florida. As the unrelenting winds thrust the surf into higher and higher waves Gena stared out at the deep green waters and angry white caps and thought, 'that's just like my life. I'm being pounded by everybody, my husband, my mother and my daughter.' The winds with specks of sand stung as they danced across her face even as the tears flowed but she still remained at the beach feeling weary and forlorn. It was well past midnight when she tiptoed into the darkened house.

At work, in spite of her distractions Gena when through her check list of chores; she inspected the completed rooms, checked if the designer pillows were fluffed properly, if the bedspreads were smoothed to perfection, if the complimentary baskets of fruit had been delivered and how the fresh flower arrangements were placed. Instead of taking the elevator to the next floor Gena trudged quietly up the back stairs and when she was within ear shot of the supply room her heart quickened. The young maids were taking a break and indoctrinating a new girl Gena had hired a few days earlier. In a flash Gena's heart skipped a beat. She realized they weren't talking or joking about some overly imbibed guest—they were talking about her.

"So is Señora Gena a pretty good boss?"

"Ah, she's OK I guess."

"Is she married?"

"Well, if you can call it that. Her husband lives in New York."

"You know, I bet he's having a ball up there, if you know what I mean." Gena grimaced when the giggling started.

"How come he's up there?"

"We don't know but can you imagine her in a bikini?"

When the laughter subsided Gena made a casual appearance and the embarrassed group scattered like birds fleeing a thunderstorm.

For weeks Gena couldn't get the conversation out of her mind. Every time she stood in front of a mirror she rehashed it over again. Perhaps she'd go and talk to her friend Jessica who ran the hotel's combined beauty parlor, massage and spa. Maybe she'd get a new hairstyle, after all she reasoned, she hadn't had a new one in years. Perhaps she'd loose some weight and buy some new clothes. And the next time Vic came for a visit he'd see how she'd changed! Christmas was several months away and she figured she had time to work on her plan.

Now Gena's life was taking on a new pattern. After dinner she'd fix a plate for her mother and afterward watch her to be sure she was swallowing her medicine. Then donning her jogging clothes she'd make her way to the beach. Many evenings as she passed along the water's edge she'd recall the things that had happened through the years along that long ribbon of sand. She smiled when she remembered her childhood and how she had enjoyed digging tunnels and building sandcastles and then under the watchful eyes of her parents she'd head to the water with her plastic bucket in tow to rinse the sand from her hands. Lying on her oversized beach towel she'd eye her mother and father hand in hand racing into the waves and floating beyond the breakers. Those years were full of security and contentment and when she grew older and her interests changed she prayed that she'd have a marriage just like her parents. But now she had to face the fact that she didn't have a marriage like her mother and father and frequently as she neared the end of her jog she'd sigh and ponder if it was always going to be like this with her in Puerto Rico and Victor miles and miles away.

Some evenings she cajoled Reva into jogging along with her and they made an attempt to reach and understand each other. Gena knew they weren't really communicating but on the surface at least they seemed to be moving in the right direction. Still she wasn't prepared for what Reva announced one evening as they moved along the water's edge.

"Mom, I want to go to New York to live with Dad. I know you're going to get mad and say I should finish school first, but that's too long to wait."

Gena swallowed hard. This wasn't going to be easy. She thought it best not to dwell on all the times Victor had disappointed his daughter telling her he was "too busy to make it home" for her birthday and she didn't want to remind her daughter of his same old lame excuses. "Things are sure to get better and I'm planning to be there for your next birthday." So deciding on another approach she asked calmly.

"Are you really sure you want to move up there now and change schools? And what about your quinceañera? We've put it off so many times at the last minute because your father couldn't make it. All your cousins had their ceremonies when they were much younger. We really need to go ahead with it and I'm sure your father will want you to have it here.

"Well, I don't care. I want to go to New York and anyway I could come back here for my quinceañera."

"And what about your friends, do you really want to up and just leave all your friends?" Gena kept thinking of what to say next to dissuade Reva but nothing seemed to be working.

"I don't have that many friends here."

Gena suspected that Max was a thing of the past so she wasn't shocked when Reva added, "Max is a dumb jerk. We broke up and I don't want to see him ever again. I want to see how Papa is living. It must be so much fun up there."

"Well, think about it some more and when he comes home for Christmas maybe we can talk to him about your moving up there."

Reva seemed placated with this arrangement and their relationship in the ensuing weeks appeared to be on more of an even keel as the young girl spoke excitedly about the clothes she'd take with her and all the new things she was sure her Papa would buy her.

As the months passed Gena's mother began a trail from her bedroom to the back yard where she sat for most of the day on an old rusty glider under a generous shade tree. She was becoming more agreeable to Gena's coaxing her to eat and swallowing her anti-depressants and while they spoke briefly about Gena's earlier outburst they didn't dwell on it. To Gena's complete surprise one night before bedtime her mother reached for her hand and spoke barely above a whisper.

"You know, Gena, you're a good daughter, maybe I deserved your outburst."

Even though Gena still felt deeply ashamed about losing her temper they put the evening behind them and never spoke of it again. Several weeks later her mother announced that she was thinking about returning to the shop where she had worked for years creating mundillos, those tatted fabrics that appear like lace and are so popular with the tourists in Puerto Rico and Spain. Gena gave her mother a hug and said a silent prayer. She felt the worst was over.

Gena's jogging continued uninterrupted. While she'd originally thought it was the best way to lose some weight and get into shape (and she was) something else was happening inside of Gena. She found that the gentle pace of the waves rushing to shore, the clear blue skies with just a hint of a wispy cloud, the familiar gulls flying above with their well-known sounds were clearing her head, giving her time to think and affording her a new perspective on her life. Thus while she'd joined the brotherhood of the sweating and panting evening runners to lose weight, she had also found a place of peace deep within herself. She was sure that Victor would approve when he returned for Christmas.

Late one afternoon Gena dropped by the hotel's elegant spa to chat with her friend Jessica. They were long-time friends. Through the years, they had enjoyed movies, seasonal festivals and special church events with their offspring tagging along. At the hotel they'd shared many cups of coffee, mulled over their family problems together and chuckled about some of their more eccentric guests. Jessica, a single mother of two had fled to Puerto Rico from Cuba several years earlier and ran the spa, massage room and beauty salon like a well-oiled machine. She was also heavily engaged with night classes at the local college and with the turn of every semester she seemed never to find a course she didn't like. More than once she'd tried to encourage Gena to accompany her and after much procrastination Gena half-heartedly agreed to try her hand at studying again. Soon the two women were heading to classes one evening a week and every other Saturday afternoon. While Jessica was breezing through a class on Sports Medicine, Gena's world was maneuvering through the principals of Basic Bookkeeping and Introduction to Computers.

One afternoon (the result of Jessica's continual coaxing), Gena presented herself for the new hair-do she had been thinking about for months. Both women were pleased with the results and there wasn't a mirror in the hotel that Gena passed that she didn't stop to admire her new look. But while the hairstyle was delightful there was something else that Gena was beginning to feel. Deep down she was feeling a sense of pride in herself.

At home Reva was in a constant state of excitement. Christmas was less than three months away and a day or two after the holiday she'd leave with her father to live in New York. Oh, life was going to be wonderful! The young teenager was constantly pouring over fashion magazines, carefully reading articles on make-up, experimenting with different hairstyles and anything else that would make her "look just right" for New York City. Amidst the chatter Gena tried to insert a note of reality.

"Have you talked this over with your father?"

"Well, no not really. I did send him e-mail but he hasn't answered it yet. Probably he's so busy.

"Perhaps you should phone him." Gena looked at Reva inquiringly and then with special emphasis added, "don't you think you should call him?"

"Well, I've left a couple of messages on his answering machine but he hasn't answered them yet." Then Reva smiled and declared, "he'll answer me, I know he will."

The following morning Gena decided to take matters into her own hands. She wanted to know when Victor would arrive in San Juan. Should she plan to meet him there or would he fly direct to Aguadilla? How long was he staying? And most of all she needed to know how he was going to handle the situation with Reva. How was he going to provide for the teenager? What school would she attend? Would he agree with her that it would be better to wait until the school year ended in May than to up-root their daughter in mid-year? All of these questions and more were thrashing around in Gena's mind. She decided she'd put it off long enough. Clutching her cell phone she strolled out onto the hotel's grounds and searched the beautiful verdant landscape for a bit of privacy. Tucked behind tall stately palm trees she spied an isolated bench near an ornamental pond filled with plump golden Japanese koi lazily weaving through fragrant water lilies. She said a silent prayer, held her breath for a minute and dialed his office.

Hearing Victor's voice made her heart beat loud and fast. Yes, he'd heard from Reva. Sure, the teenager might be able to come up to New York. Yes, he'd try to make it down there for Christmas and then they'd talk about Reva's move. That was all Gena needed to hear. He was coming home for Christmas! If she had listened more carefully she might have noticed that Vic's voice was totally devoid of enthusiasm. Instead of a defined "sure I'll be there for the holiday," he had inserted a half-hearted probably. Nor did she notice that he had said "Reva can come up for a visit rather than what the young girl was dreaming of, a permanent move and a new school. Before Gena had time to question him further he announced curtly he was already late for a conference and couldn't talk any longer. But Gena was uplifted and she was happy for Reva. In spite of what Reva wanted surely they could talk it out and plan for their daughter to stay in Puerto Rico until she graduated from school. But all that could wait. Victor was coming home for Christmas! It was going to be a spectacular Christmas this year! Perhaps. Perhaps not.

Several evenings later Jessica, Gena and Reva arrived at the local mall with purses filled with credit cards, checks and cash. They were bent on a mission. As the evening wore on dresses, jeans, shoes, sweaters and a coat for Reva were stuffed into over-sized shopping bags. Winters in Puerto Rico are mild and pleasant and for Reva, who'd never had a heavy coat before, the novelty was almost overwhelming. She insisted in visiting every store in the mall that carried winter garb at least twice and tried on coat after coat, scouring the racks for just "the right one." Near closing time Gena and Jessica were worn out, they felt they couldn't move another inch. But finally their patience paid off. Reva found the "coolest coat" and they left the mall tired but happy. As the bags were being piled into the car Jessica spoke of a special flimsy black negligee she'd spotted. At first Gena ignored her but the more she thought of it . . . A few minutes later she ran back to the store. The black nightgown was wrapped and carried to the car amidst giggles from Reva and winks from Jessica.

"Maybe you guys could spend a night in the hotel, take advantage of the spa and who knows . . . .?" Jessica took the wheel, the car edged out of the parking log and Reva chatted ceaselessly about her new clothes. Gena's thoughts stayed with the black negligee in a white box on her lap.

* * *

The alarm was about to ring but Carol was already stirring in the large spacious bed, in the large spacious bedroom of the large spacious apartment on New York's upper West Side. She focused on the figure beside her. How did she ever let this guy really get to her? She who had spent much of her time drifting from affair to affair with no serious attachments, with no serious distractions, focusing always first and foremost on her career. But she couldn't fight it any longer. She loved him. Actually she loved everything about him. His loving ways, his generosity, his success, his dark swarthy looks and most impressive, how he could shift into his fun loving attitude after an intense day at one of New York's prestigious international banks. He certainly hadn't let any grass grow under his feet. From the time he'd arrived in New York he'd begun his climb up the corporate ladder, albeit slowly at times and not without struggling over some obstacles, but he was nearing the top now. And all Carol could think of was spending the rest of her life with him. She had it all planned. Christmas would be extra special this year. They'd go skiing in Vermont near her family's cabin and one evening around a crackling fire they'd look to the year ahead. They had often spoke of making their relationship permanent but hadn't really pinned down a date yet. They had also talked of Vic's promise to fix his "island problem" which was his way of referring to his long-distance marriage that hadn't been a real marriage in a long time. Carol moved closer and ran her hands over Victor's bare chest. When she rubbed her knee next to his bare thigh he stirred and took her in his arms. Mornings were supposed to be like this Carol thought and the couple melted into each other and shut out the day's problems.

Later in the shower together they laid out their day. Meet for lunch if their busy schedules permitted, if not, grab a taxi after work and arrive at one of their favorite restaurants for drinks and dinner. Life was good they admitted to themselves as they both hailed cabs and sped along Madison Avenue in different directions. Vic's thoughts stayed with Carol. He thought about her quick smile, her congenial personality, her perfectly shaped body, warm and open to him no matter the time of day or night. Her long chestnut colored hair and sparkling blue-green eyes accentuated her fair skin and when she accompanied him to a business function she had the admiring glances of the crowd. Victor entered the bank's elegant lobby and made his way to his impressive oak-paneled office. He was unaware that a phone call this morning would send his life into a tailspin.

Carol's office phone was already buzzing when she arrived at her desk. It would be another hectic day but it was the price of the career she had carved out for herself. For several years she had been a dedicated and hard working talent scout and it was a well-known fact that Carol Peterson was the agent to have on your side if you were attempting a show business career. One of her clients was presently rehearsing for an off-Broadway opening already touted to be the hit the year, while others were living the good life with perks from their successful daytime soaps or other television endeavors. Several high-powered deals were pending and this morning she was picking up a client and dropping the young actress-to-be at an open casting call. Carol's career was at the highest it had been in years. She had been lucky of course; she had learned the business at her father's knee and he had inherited the agency from her grandfather whom she adored. It was no surprise when she answered the phone to hear her grandfather's voice. He called frequently and lost no opportunity to tell her how proud he was of her and her accomplishments.

"Gramps, I've got something great to tell you."

"What is it, another client hitting the great white way?"

"Well, no, this is something different. I'm really, finally and completely in love."

"Wonderful, and who is this lucky guy?"

"I'll tell you more about it when we see you." She took a sip of her morning coffee before continuing. "Oh, Gramps, I'm so happy, so completely happy."

"Well, you guys are going to make it out here for Thanksgiving I hope, and we are all going to be together for Christmas, aren't we?"

"Sure, we wouldn't miss it for the world."

The conversation continued with rapid-fire questions from her grandfather. By the time they finished talking, Gramps had learned everything he wanted to know about Victor D'Arrezzo. At least he thought he knew everything.

Slowly sipping a steaming cup of coffee Victor lingered near his large window affording a full-view of New York's inspiring skyline. He could barely

see the cars racing up and down and the specks of people scurrying about below but it didn't matter what he saw. His mind was elsewhere. Tonight would
be special. He had planned everything down to the last detail. A jeweler friend
was dropping over shortly before he left for the day with an exquisite engagement ring and tonight amid champagne and flowers he'd slip the ring on
Carol's finger and they'd officially announce their engagement to her large
family on Christmas day when they were all together skiing in Vermont. As
if to jar him back to reality the buzz of the phone pulled him to his desk. A
few minutes later he slumped in his chair and put the telephone down. The remainder of the day was hell. Gena's call from Puerto Rico couldn't have
come at a worst time. He hadn't solved the "island problem" before now and
that procrastination would haunt him in the days ahead.

The small and intimate Little Italy restaurant was a delight. Their favorite
cozy out of the way table promised to lead to a wonderful evening. Outside
the snowflakes were falling heavier now and the whole city was taking on a
special pre-holiday atmosphere. However, storm clouds were forming in
more places than in the sky.

It had began romantically enough. Carol appeared radiant as she starred
teary-eyed at her sparkling diamond. After a few glasses of Dom Perignon
Victor nervously dropped his bombshell. It looked as if he'd have to forgo
their trip to Vermont. His wife and daughter wanted him in Puerto Rico for
the holiday. His daughter was finally having her overdue quinceañera. Carol
looked at her lover aghast. Then as if an after thought, Victor admitted sheepishly, no, he hadn't taken care of his "island problem" yet.

"You told me last summer you were taking care of it."

"Yeah I know, but it I just let it slide and hell, I didn't think it would come
up and change our plans for Christmas. It's just a technicality anyway."

"A technicality? A technicality? It's me, it's us. You're going down there to
see your wife and you call it a technicality? Oh, you bastard."

They fell silent for the moment then Carol jumped up and grabbed Victor's
glass before repeating, "You bastard." Her voice was shaky when she spoke.
"All this time I thought you were free and clear of your marriage."

The next thing Victor noticed was that his plate of linguini was swimming
in champagne.

Outside Carol disappeared into the darkness letting the heavy flakes of
snow hit her face and blend with her tears. At the apartment she popped into
a hot bubble bath and slid between the satin sheets but not before flinging her
ring in the corner of the night stand drawer and stopping to lock the guest
room door. Today had been the worst day of her life.

Thanksgiving was fast approaching. Carol's family had always considered
the day a prelude to Christmas and decorations began to appear throughout

the house. However, Carol was too upset to even think of the holidays. There'd be no tree this year, no apartment decorations, no attending parties together. She spent more and more time at the office and after a busy day she'd grab a bite to eat before arriving home and going straight to bed, alone. Victor and her headed for the Hamptons Thanksgiving morning and although they hadn't spoken much since that night at the restaurant they attempted to put on a happy face. It didn't work. The day was a disaster. While her grandfather wasn't in the know about his granddaughter's "island problem" he felt as if something wasn't going well. But the more he observed the young couple he decided it might be just a lover's quarrel and thought it best not to say anything at the moment. If things didn't seem to improve by Christmas then he'd demand to know the truth.

One evening after dinner as Carol cleared the plates in silence (one of the many such evenings during the past weeks) Victor came up behind her and took her in his arms.

"Baby, listen to me. I can't lose you. I'm not going to Puerto Rico. We can go on with our plans just like before. Vermont. The whole bit. I called my daughter today. And then I called an old college friend of mine who is a lawyer in San Juan. He is taking care of the divorce papers. He's sending the preliminary papers out tomorrow."

Carol stood perfectly still.

"Baby, I'm telling you. The papers will be here and you can see for yourself." Then he added as he pulled her closer. "I'm sorry I let you down. It was stupid of me to let it slide. I want us to be married more than anything."

Over a few glasses of Pinot Noir they talked for what seemed hours before pulling down a few suitcases and beginning to pack for their skiing trip to Vermont later in the week.

* * *

Gena heard the cries before she slipped the key in the lock. Something terrible must have happened. Her first thought was her mother. Did she fall? Did she have a heart attack? In a split second she dashed to her mother's room and stopped short. The sobs were coming from Reva's bedroom! The young girl was lying face down on the bed, pounding her pillow, screaming and ignoring the pleas of her grandmother. Reva, her face flushed bright red and swollen looked up and shot her mother a fleeting glance before collapsing into her pillow to resume her muffled screeching.

"Papa's not coming home for Christmas."

The rest of the evening was like walking in a hazy cloud. Finally Gena got her daughter calmed down enough to talk. Victor had called that afternoon.

No, he wasn't able to make it for Christmas or for her quinceañera. He even suggested putting the ceremony off until May when he'd be there "for sure." Gena held her daughter and remembered all the disappointments, all the broken promises through the years. They sat huddled together, crying for each other and crying for themselves for most of the night. The next morning Reva begged off school, Gena begged off work. The elderly widow, the mother and the daughter, all three of them needed each other and needed to be together. Each of them was dealing with their emotional scars in a different way but as Christmas neared they agreed that they needed to move on to their old and fast traditions.

Soon a Christmas tree stood in one corner of the front room banked with bright red poinsettias and their much-loved pesebres, those old treasured nativity scenes that remain in the family for generations. The kitchen took on a new flurry of activity, the oven held large slabs of roasting pork, a large pot of seasoned rice and pigeon peas was making gentle hissing noises on the stove alongside another simmering cast iron container of green bananas. While Gena and her mother mashed plantains and added the mixture to meat before wrapping all in banana tree leaves, Reva was laboring over a pan of turrón, working the white nougat and almonds that had been her favorite since childhood. After attending midnight mass, the traditional Misa de Gallo, they exchanged gifts and shed a few tears. All was ready for their Christmas dinner when family and friends dropped by.

The house was full of chattering and smiling relatives and friends from morning to night and Jessica found it difficult to speak to Gena alone. What was wrong with her? Certainly Gena didn't look like her old self. And where was Victor? When the two women had a few private moments Gena, trying desperately to hold back tears emptied her soul. The week had been a nightmare. After Victor's call she'd used every bit of her energy to buoy up her daughter and her mother, more often than not, unsuccessfully. Then a lawyer called and made an appointment to meet her a week later. She knew the inevitable. Her marriage was over. Jessica was in shock. Sure she knew the marriage hadn't been the best, but a divorce?

"After all you've done for him, your new hair style, losing weight, going to college, how could he do this to you? Now the SOB won't even see what you've done for him."

They hugged and Jessica left with a "you know I'm here for you, anytime."

New Year's came and went and in spite of all the festivities Gena was still aching and the trip to the lawyer's office didn't help. She signed the preliminary papers and the divorce began its slow roll through the courts. If only she could forget Jessica's statement. It was churning through her head when she rode the hotel elevator up and down, when she checked the supplies, when she reprimanded or praised her staff, when she changed into her jogging clothes and made it down to the beach. There it was, that same gnawing sentence "after all you've done for him" over and over darting through her mind. The more she thought of it the more ridiculous the statement sounded. Finding a spot on the sand and sitting and hugging her knees she gazed out onto the surf and admitted to herself, sure at first I fooled myself into thinking that I was making myself more attractive, more interesting for Victor. But I wasn't really doing it for him. I was doing it all for ME. I've grown and I've changed for ME! For ME!

Gena had made a monumental step forward. She'd discovered the person inside her she never really knew existed. Who can discount that feeling of pride and joy one can have in oneself?

* * *

May is a beautiful month in Puerto Rico. The gentle breezes off the water dance across the island bringing sunny days and cool temperatures with little danger of tropical storms that can effect the area from June through November. Tourist traffic is heavy but the two women making their way through the crowded terminal were not waiting for just any tourist. They were ready to meet a person out of their past. Reva had long since stopped hating her father for all the disappointments, for all the canceled trips, even for her never-to-be quinceañera. Everyone had decided that at eighteen she had been a woman for several years and it would be inappropriate to have the ceremony at this late date. She was graduating from school in a few hours and had her sights set on college. Gena now had an assistant due to the hotel chain's huge expansion and along with her busy job she had increased her college load and was now on a degree plan. She had long since reached the point where she could think of Victor without hurting and the future never looked brighter.

The striking couple walked through the terminal and attempted awkward introductions and handshakes. Gena gave Carol the once over and caught the same coming from Carol. Victor spoke of the reception he and his new wife had planned for Reva following her graduation ceremony that afternoon. The evening went well. Father and daughter danced. For pictures mother and father danced but said little. Finally Victor faced Gena in a quiet spot at the bar. She had felt his eyes on her all evening and more than once had wondered what he was seeing. Over a glass of rum splashed with coconut milk he reached for Gena's hand.

"You sure look great."

"Thank you, I feel great!"

"You look so different," then awkwardly he added, " I wonder if I ever really knew you."

Deep inside Gena wondered if the same wasn't also true for her. Had she ever really known this man, this man who she had dated all through her teen years, had married according to their families' expectations and had a child? Victor's next words brought her back to reality.

"Gena, I think we got married too young. We were just two kids infatuated with each other but believed we were in love, the kind of love that lasts a lifetime."

Gena looked deep into Victor's eyes. "You know, maybe this is the first thing we have agreed on in many years. Anyway, thanks for coming for your daughter. We should remain friends for her sake."

The next afternoon they all arrived at the airport and watched the plane become a tiny speck in the sky. Victor and Carol were returning to their busy lives and as Gena and Reva headed back home, Gena suggested that her daughter plan a visit to her father and new stepmother sometime in the near future.

"Well, maybe someday but for now I'm happy to stay here, to get started in college and get a career." Reva rested her hand on her mother's arm and continued. "And Mama you don't need to worry. I know I'm too young to jump into marriage any time soon. I see all the heartache it brought for you." And as an afterthought, "and for Papa."

The small dark blue sedan on the ribbon of road winding towards the beach stopped and two women emerged and raced towards the water's edge. Facing the wind and considering what they had been through, they looked forward to their new lives confident that they could meet any challenge that life handed them.

Index